Virtual Summit Launch Formula

The Secret Way To Grow Your Business, Build Your Community & Increase Your Influence Online — And Get Paid To Do It

Eric Z. Yang

Copyright © Eric Z. Yang
All Rights Reserved.

Special Gifts For Readers

By purchasing this book, you've gained access to 3 exclusive bonuses to help you launch a successful virtual summit:

1) A-to-Z Virtual Summit Checklist

2) Profitable Summit Worksheet

3) The Winning Sponsorship Deck Used to Raise $75,000 USD (despite not having an email list)

Head here to claim them:

Leadnextgen.com/book-bonus

Table of Contents

Introduction	5
Chapter 1: How 1 Book, 1 Event, 1 Person Saved My Life	12
- Childhood Entrepreneurship	
- The Path from Depression	
- Trial and Error to Ultimate Success	
Chapter 2: Should You Host A Virtual Summit?	18
- Search for Your Why	
- 7 Reasons Why Virtual Summits are Game Changers	
- Why Now is the Best Time	
Chapter 3: Myths Debunked	30
- The 7 Limiting Beliefs Holding You Back Right Now	
Chapter 4: The Proof	37
- Millennial Success Summit (Broker)	
- Airbnb Mastery Summit (Expert)	
- Crypto Virtual Summit (Reporter)	
Chapter 5: 6 Mistakes Summit Hosts Make	44
- How You Might Be Ruining Your Reputation & Growth Without Knowing It	
Chapter 6: How To Pick Your Summit Theme	51
- What Are You Passionate About?	
- Research Top Podcasts in Different Niches	
- Popular Online Course	
- Amazon Books	

Chapter 7: Does the Market Need Your Summit? 61
- Research Other Summits
- Your Customer Avatar

Chapter 8: How to Profit From Your Summit 66
- Research Industry Leaders
- How to Create Your Summit Offer

Chapter 9: Summit Name and Hook 70
- Define the Audience
- Define the Benefits
- Write 10 and Choose 3

Chapter 10: Finding & Booking Your Speakers 73
- Why Having Influencers Matters
- Types of Influencers to Have
- Where to Find Your Influencers
- Strategies to Book Your Dream Speaker
- Steps After Confirming Speakers

Chapter 11: Setting Up Your Virtual Summit Funnel 81
- Registration Page
- Opt-in Page
- Thank You & Sales Page
- Checkout Page
- Inner-pages
- Support Page
- Membership Page
- Quality Control Everything

Chapter 12: Getting Sponsors 97
- The Offer

- The Prospects
- The Outreach
- The Deal

Chapter 13: How to Run Your Summit   108
- Pre-launch
- Launch
- Post-launch

Chapter 14: Post-Summit   121
- Offering Upsells
- Offering Downsells
- Make it Evergreen
- Relaunching

Chapter 15: Conclusion   131

Introduction

You probably picked up this book because you're hungry to create something that provides real value to people and to the world.

Maybe you're also interested in generating income in a more sustainable and strategic way than following the 9-to-5 lifestyle.

Maybe you've spent a tremendous amount of time searching for the right community filled with like-minded entrepreneurs— but failed to find a place you can call home.

Maybe you've also considered or started becoming a speaker, coach, or leader of a tribe— but you haven't seen much success in these areas either.

Maybe you've failed so many times that you're wondering if it's just you that can't be successful. Or maybe you think you're doing something wrong but can't identify exactly what.

Or maybe, you already have some level of success and you want the best strategy to grow your business, but failed to find a proven system for building community and authority.

If these pains sound oddly familiar, I can honestly tell you that I've been in your shoes.

I read every book I could get my hands on and absorbed all the advice I could from "gurus" and "experts", but they just didn't give me the actionable steps I needed.

All this studying left me dazed and confused. There were so many "magic pills" and paths to success. I easily spent over $50,000 in training,

masterminds, and courses, but they would all either contradict each other or took my focus away from what I really should have been doing.
The "shiny object syndrome" was real. Unfortunately, my bank account wasn't looking as bright.

Some books and course mentors advised me to teach what I learned— but I didn't want to teach things that didn't even work for me.

I kept wandering around until I learned something that would change everything.

How top experts and thought leaders first started building their influence and fortune.

How Tony Robbins, Tim Ferriss, and even Russell Brunson earned respect when they first started— and ultimately became thought leaders while impacting millions across the world.
The foundation of their respective empires was built on one principle:

→ **Broadcasting knowledge and owning a platform to spread this information to the world.**

The best part is, if you aren't an expert or lack experience in your field, you can become a knowledge broker or reporter.

The information doesn't necessarily need to come from your mouth. You can interview experts on your platform and get the answers to questions you've had for years.

As long as the quality is great— that's what matters most to the audience. And you'll benefit immensely from being associated with all the greats of your industry, which will increase your authority without having to "fake it".

Tim Ferriss started out as a reporter by interviewing billionaires and world-class practitioners on his podcast.

Tony Robbins' first in-person conference was done as a knowledge broker where he taught his audience the framework that his mentor Jim Rohn gave him.

Russell Brunson learned how to build a potato gun and became a known expert by selling that information on his first webinar.

What's the point here?
Podcasts. Events. Webinars.

If you want to systematically grow your tribe, your influence, and your revenue, those platforms are typically what most would advise you to do.

It has helped the industry titans create solid foundations when they first started many years ago.

But the market has changed.

The truth is:
- **In-person events build authority but are unscalable**
- **Webinars grow your email list but have low perceived value**
- **Podcasting is remote but doesn't generate revenue**

If you tried any of those 3 platforms and failed (or didn't achieve the success you expected), it's completely normal.

People have become used to getting an upsell after a webinar, and they don't care about your PDF book anymore. Everyone's talking about how you should start a podcast to build authority. Unless you're a superhuman like Nathan Latka, only .01% generate revenue from it.

This is crazy!

Competition has exponentially grown over time and it's become way harder to market yourself now than 5 years ago.

At the same time. the knowledge industry is a **$355 million a day** business. In five years, Forbes expects it to be a billion dollar a day industry. Easily.

Tony Robbins shared that only 27% of people actually work in jobs that they went to school for, and more than half of them are miserable in their jobs. Employers are looking for specialized education, not the generalized material that colleges offer. College debt is cripplingly high.

The world needs more practical and updated information.

You don't want to miss out on this train, and it's necessary to have a platform that can be easily scalable, high in revenue, and profitable to support your business growth.

But most people don't know how to do it.

It's about **working smarter, not harder**. There's no need to spend years experimenting to find what actually works, especially not when people (like me) have already taken one for the team and done the hard work for you.

That's how I stumbled upon virtual summits.

They achieve all the benefits of a webinar, in-person event, and podcast—without any of the downsides.

WHAT IS A VIRTUAL SUMMIT & HOW CAN IT HELP ME?

Maybe you're not familiar with this term yet, but you're about to be.

A virtual summit is **an online event platform that gathers experts to teach the audience everything they need to know about a specific industry.**

Summits offer incredible value in knowledge-sharing and live interaction, which is one of the most powerful growth tools. They are capable of rapidly building your authority and expanding both the quantity and quality of key relationships, as well as generating large-scale income.

All of this can be achieved by pivoting to virtual summits.

They take all the proven benefits and best aspects of a live event, webinar, *and* podcast wrapped together in one.

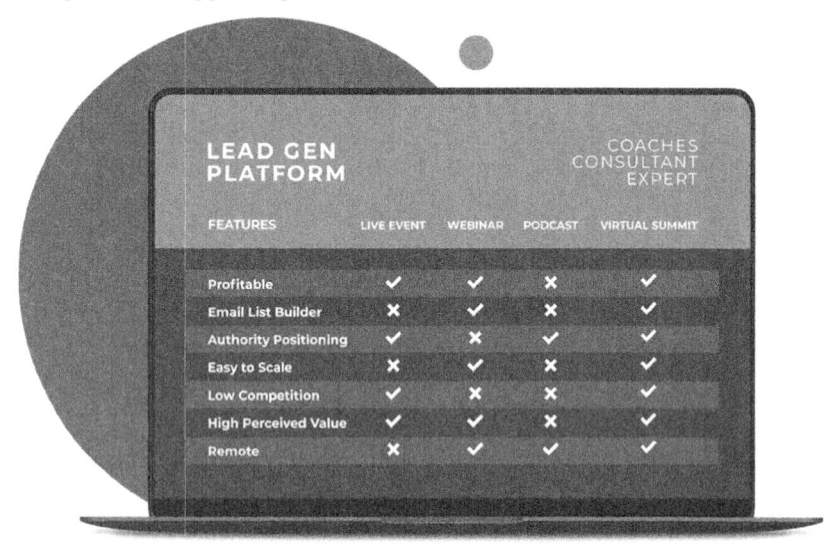

LEAD GEN PLATFORM				COACHES CONSULTANT EXPERT
FEATURES	LIVE EVENT	WEBINAR	PODCAST	VIRTUAL SUMMIT
Profitable	✓	✓	✗	✓
Email List Builder	✗	✓	✗	✓
Authority Positioning	✓	✗	✓	✓
Easy to Scale	✗	✓	✗	✓
Low Competition	✓	✗	✗	✓
High Perceived Value	✓	✓	✗	✓
Remote	✗	✓	✓	✓

By offering valuable content in the most high-performing way, you'll access advantages that **you wouldn't believe**, starting with:

- Fast-tracked growth of your business by establishing yourself as an industry authority while achieving widespread visibility

- A quickly-built strong community that generates recurring clients and an ever-growing audience
- Exponentially increased influence— which you can use to move forward in whatever market you choose

These things are the **hardest to achieve but also the most rewarding**. Major leaders and speakers are still working tirelessly to obtain and maintain them. It's totally attainable.

And **a virtual summit is the way to do it**.

In this book, I will show you the virtual summit launch formula that I used to generate over $350,000 in less than 2 years— gathering over 35,000 attendees across my personal events.
This proven system has been used by my agency and clients that I've personally consulted, producing very similar results.

I'm also going to debunk some common myths about hosting a virtual summit. Myths that you've definitely heard and that you probably even believe about yourself.

These myths are the core reasons you're still struggling with your business. They're holding you back from success and freedom that you deserve.

When it comes to hosting and launching a virtual summit, the first step we'll take is discovering why you want to do one in the first place. Then we will strategize your summit theme and explore how to get your first speakers.

You also get the blueprint to create your inner-pages and the step-by-step process to fund your summit through sponsorship.

Finally, you also access the checklist for your summit launch to ensure that everything goes smoothly (get it on leadnextgen.com/book-bonus)

I wrote this book to encompass everything I would have wanted and needed to fast-track myself to success from the very start, and that's exactly what it's designed to do for you.

Virtual summits gave me the financial freedom and location independence that I dreamt of. And it has helped countless leading entrepreneurs launch and scale their businesses to the next level and beyond.

All you need to do now is keep reading and find out how you can do it too.

Chapter 1: How 1 Book, 1 Event, 1 Person Saved My Life

In this section you are going to learn:

- How I pulled myself out of depression for good
- How I finally crafted the ultimate virtual summit blueprint
- How it's possible to grow your tribe, build influence, and generate more revenue without the risks & drawbacks

---

You're probably wondering how a guy like me ended up as an expert in the world of virtual summits.

And let's be clear, it didn't happen easily. I went through the challenges, desperate moments, and repeated trial and error before finding the formula that works. And now I want to share it so you don't have to.

Born and raised in Paris, I had my first taste of entrepreneurship at 7 years old by selling imported goods to my schoolmates. I would spend every summer in China and brought along a half-empty suitcase to fill with objects I could sell.

I sold endless items but my bestseller was video games. I would 15x my return but provided massive value to customers since my offer was still $30 cheaper for them than most video game store prices there.

Another absolute best-selling item was Nintendo DS cartridges. I offered 5 of them for the price of 1 with a special cartridge that could hold more capacity. Since most in-store options only had 1 game per cartridge, my 5-in-1 offer was a no-brainer.

The entrepreneurship spirit hit me early on, but so did depression.

Everything seemed fine on the surface but I was dying on the inside. I felt terribly lost, misunderstood, and even suicidal.

All depression is different, but this is what mine looked like.

I cried for no reason. Grieved for nothing and everything. Thoughts like *I can't do this, why am I alone, I don't have anyone to talk to, I can't do this anymore* were my daily reminders. I cried these words out loud, too.

And then there were moments of joy. Feeling free and hoping the next day would lift all the mental and physical numbness away. But every night would be a new disappointment..

Soon enough, the dark thoughts would come back to remind me that my life wasn't nearly where I wanted it to be. And I felt like there was nothing I could do to fight it.

I laid on my floor a lot, not feeling anything. Not even hunger, despite being 6'2 and weighing less than 100 pounds at the time.

I was just deliriously exhausted, constantly feeling like I'd been up for days. I would usually drop out of sight for days or weeks. Not going to school or seeing people.

I even flew to another country in an attempt to escape the depression, thinking that a new school, new environment, new friends, new girlfriend would help me get better— and of course it didn't. My environment wasn't the problem; the source of my sadness was within.

And honestly, I had no particular reason to be depressed— I had the basics of what I needed to live a satisfied life. But I felt so deeply unsatisfied with the path ahead of me.

Getting good grades. Getting into a good school. Getting a good internship. Presumably, all this would lead to a good job, salary, and ultimately waiting for retirement before you know it.

That future life made me mentally sick— but I didn't know what I could do to evade it.

But one person, one book, and one event changed everything.

I randomly stumbled upon Tony Robbins' *Unlimited Power* in a bookstore, and something just clicked as I was reading it.

The act of ending the blame game and taking full responsibility for everything that happens in my life helped me more in 2 days than the 2 years of antidepressants ever did.

I knew I was at a turning point of my life... the choice was either staying where I was or investing in myself.

So I used my life savings (17 years of untouched Christmas & birthday money)— and flew to another continent in the middle of the school week to attend Tony's event in Los Angeles.

Over the course of a weekend, he taught over 10,000 attendees how to create a winning mindset and how to use that energy to fuel your aspirations— even if you didn't know what it would be yet, you had the tools to find the solutions.

This event *saved my life* and made me decide to move to the United States to continue my personal education.

I touched down in Southern California and picked a community college to get quick classes, investing the majority of my tuition money into attending over 30 events within the first year alone. I loved every minute of it, but there was one recurring problem: **I just couldn't find any entrepreneurs who weren't at least twice my age.**

Tired of not finding young entrepreneurs, I decided to build my dream event to attract them.

My first event gathered over 100 entrepreneurs and generated 6 figures. It was an incredible feeling but there was still one major problem:

> *Live events are an amazing growth hack to build your authority, relationships, and income, but are* ***the worst when it comes to scalability***.

Think about it.

You spend 6 months getting speakers, sponsors, and attendees for your event, pay high prices for a venue, and then once the event ends, everything disappears and you need to restart the process all over again.

If you don't have an existing email list or audience, there are also *tremendous risks* to hosting an event with the upfront costs.

The truth is that despite generating 6 figures, I barely broke even on my first event (a lot of gurus claim they *make* 6 figures... but hide the 6-figure expenses).

I was still struggling and didn't know what my next move would be.

This was when I met a young entrepreneur named Chandler Bolt, who was barely 21 years old but already making huge moves in his industry. After talking, I learned that he launched a virtual summit on Amazon self-publishing which generated over $370,000 plus 30,000 new subscribers for his business.

It blew my mind how a simple online conference could **generate so much income without much overhead cost**. (At the time of writing this book, Chandler's company generates around 400k per month— thanks to the foundation his virtual summit has built for his business.)

Since meeting Chandler, I've helped launch countless virtual summits ranging from Airbnb to Cryptocurrencies, passing by Amazon drop-shipping, Media, and Productivity.

All the online events we've helped systematically launch had over 7,000 attendees and generated close to 6 figures in profit, despite not always having any existing lists or connections with industry leaders. Most of them didn't even have an email list.

This takes the best of all worlds— *Live Event + Webinar + Podcast—* without any of its cons.

We've also cracked the code on how anyone can get paid and be profitable before their virtual summit even launches (hint: sponsorships done right).

But I am also writing this book so that anyone can systematically **grow their tribe, build their influence, and generate more revenue for their business.**

And if you don't have a business or summit theme in mind yet, this book is the blueprint you've been waiting for to host a profitable event.

By mistake at first, I eventually created a fail-safe and tested system for finding and launching a profitable virtual summit. And with each refinement, I made it better and better. To my surprise, following the system that I created, my summits got exponentially greater results over time.

This system is exactly what I'll be teaching you throughout the rest of this book. I'll walk you through the process step-by-step.

What you will learn in the following chapters is **the same system that I use for my high-ticket virtual summit agency**. My clients pay me over $30K to get the system you are about to receive.

If a college dropout with no connections can do it, so can you.

Chances are you have some doubts. Everyone has doubts and limiting beliefs. These beliefs and fears often keep people from starting their own projects or from finishing them. But they don't have to.

In the next chapters, I'm going to address these doubts, fears, limiting beliefs, and plain old myths head-on. I'll show you how to reverse these negative beliefs and turn them into positive drivers that will give you the confidence to write or launch your summit by finding your Why.

I'll also show you how to tackle some of the biggest myths when it comes to launching your first summit. These myths keep people from starting because **they're convinced the process is much harder and more time consuming than it actually is**. It doesn't have to be.

Chapter 2: Should You Host A Virtual Summit?

In this section you are going to learn:
- How to define your true purpose
- Why virtual summits are changing the game for good— to your benefit
- Why *Now* is your best entrance point

Search For Your Why

When people come up to me and ask if they should host a summit, I always ask questions about their ultimate outcome:

What is your purpose? What are your goals? Where do you want to go with this project?

It can't be a short answer like *"Because someone else launched a successful virtual summit"* or *"Because I want to build my email list"*.

Sorry, but those answers aren't good enough.
Everything that you do needs to serve a very clear purpose.

When we onboard a new virtual summit client, we spend hours nailing down the purpose behind each launch— the thing that is going to drive you to the finish line. If you don't have a goal, how do you expect to score?

If you want to inspire others, always be clear on your why first.

In his book *Start With Why,* Simon Sinek makes it clear that businesses and individuals who want to achieve fulfilment and profits need to be clear on their *Why*.

Every single company and organization on the planet knows WHAT they do. Some companies and people know HOW they do what they do. But **only a few people or companies can clearly articulate WHY** they do what they do.

Next to your end goal, you must clearly articulate your why and purpose for creating your virtual summit. Those two factors make up the foundation for everything else that rests on it.

Once you have solid answers to these questions, you will find it easier to articulate your ideas into a *profitable* summit blueprint.

The purpose behind your summit could be anything from connecting with influencers, building a tribe to spread a message, becoming an authority figure in your niche, or creating a platform to upsell your high-end programs to gain more clients who need your services.

Whatever it might be, it has to be something *beyond making money.* If the primary driver is to make money, it's a weak reason to do anything. It won't fuel or discipline you for the next couple months working on this project.

---

7 BENEFITS OF HOSTING A VIRTUAL SUMMIT

After working with many entrepreneurs on their summits, I discovered that most typically fall into at least one of those 7 categories.

You want more than one benefit to your summit, but I would recommend picking only 1 main goal and make it your North Star for the rest of your launch. This way you won't be distracted from your summit *Why*.

1. Expanding Your Network

Is there any influencer, entrepreneur, or personality you dream of talking to? Or even certain people you'd like to work with but don't know how to approach them via cold email?

Hosting virtually gives you leverage to interview literally anyone in the world, similar to a podcast. And for a speaker to say yes, it is all about presenting the value of being featured on the summit that brings together their ideal audience.

You can even interview big A-type speakers if timing is right. Do your research and see if that person has any launch coming soon. They might be looking for an additional platform to share their message or project with the world.

Virtual summits add value by introducing that speaker in front of your ideal audience. In his eyes, you are doing most of the heavy lifting by gathering an audience to watch his interview.

Most of the speakers on my first summit were reached via cold email. And I've become very close friends with a handful of speakers— even travelled the world and shared a stage in front of hundreds of attendees.

2. Building Social Proof

One great benefit from hosting a virtual summit is *positioning yourself in the center of big names*. This strategically puts you around great names, companies, and influencers in your industry.
Even though you might not be the expert or the one teaching and sharing on the summit, you are the one that brought those amazing names under one roof.

Even if attendees don't know who you are, **you will be the person they trust the most by the end of the summit**. As the host, you benefit the most from this association because attendees will automatically think you are equally if not *more* influential than your summit speakers. Insane, right?

This is why it is important to get what I call an **Anchor Speaker:** a famous or respected personality that will attract other speakers and attendees to be part of the conference.

Getting the Tony Robbins or Gary Vaynerchuk of your industry can be a huge selling point for attracting more speakers, since they'll also want to associate their names with industry leaders and will quickly sense the competition.

3. List Building
Virtual summits are the best way to capture cheap leads. Period.

Podcasts and YouTube channels don't offer the same functionality because they want to retrain the audience on their platforms.

E-books, webinars, or free blueprints aren't effective lead magnets anymore. Virtual summits create a hype by giving up to 30+ hours of content for free in exchange of an email.

'The gold is in the list' is an expression that a lot of online marketers use because it's still the most effective way to communicate with your entire community.

It's even more relevant today as social media can be a great platform to share content and reach new audiences, but Facebook, Linkedin, YouTube, and Instagram *increasingly limit organic reach.* They want you to pay to get access to your own community.

I'm sure you must feel like you're getting fewer likes and comments than a couple years ago. And it's not in your head, it's because it's true.

If you have 10K followers on Facebook or Instagram, only a fraction of your own followers are even going to see new content unless you're willing to pay for it— and this cost compounds over time.

When you have an email list, **you control the entire access to your audience.** There are no gatekeepers and you can be 100% sure that the email you sent will show up in their inbox.

That's how Kevin Hart built his entire comedy empire— by having his own email list.

Kevin Hart tours were the highest grossing comedy tour ever reported to Billboard Boxscore and he was the 2nd highest paid comedian in 2018.

And he started his business and brand all by building his email list....

Not a coincidence.

At the beginning of every show, an assistant would put a business card on each seat at every table that read, "Kevin Hart needs to know who you are," and asked for their email address.

After the show, his team would collect the cards and enter the names into a spreadsheet organized by location.

For 4 years he toured the country this way, building an enormous database of loyal fans and drawing more and more people to every subsequent show.

This asset is so unusual in Hollywood that it actually became controversial when Hart began to leverage it.

Negotiations between Sony and Hart's representatives were heated because, unlike other actors, Kevin had direct access to his audience and constantly asked for higher pay in exchange for granting others access to his loyal community.

This infuriated Sony, which seemed to think it was entitled to what Hart built and controlled.

Kevin responded with: "I worked very hard to get where I am today. I look at myself as a brand and because of that I will never allow myself to be taken advantage of."

If his movie career were to suddenly implode, Kevin Hart would still make a killing on the road, because he knows exactly *who you are* and what city to come perform for his audience without having to rely on an agency or studio to supply this information.

The lesson here is to never be overly dependent on a platform or entity. And **the best way to ensure complete control is by building an email list**. It's the only communication tool that is truly your own.

4. Revenue

In my interview with Jordan Harbinger, host of the *Art of Charm* podcast with over 2.5M downloads per month, I was curious to know more about the business model of podcasting.

I wanted to know whether it was an oversaturated industry, if it was still worth it for newcomers to jump on the podcast train, and more importantly for me to learn how to actually make money from podcasting.

I vividly remember Jordan saying:

→ "Please please please. For the love of god, do not start a podcast".

But then he walked me through the math of launching a podcast: "There are over 500,000 active podcasts, and if you're lucky, you'll only have around 500 to 1,000 podcasts that you are in direct competition with".

"On average, 500 podcasts are launched every single day, so you're competing with newcomers as well, so it doesn't make much sense to launch a podcast if you are trying to make money from it".

Gary Vaynerchuk talks a lot about audio and how everyone should launch their own podcast. He also shares how most people should not monetize their audience and instead should keep curating their tribe by constantly sharing great value.

You kinda build authority but don't make any money. Cool.

Jordan Harbinger went deeper when he explained that podcasts are a great tool to build a network and social proof, but you won't generate revenue unless you're in the top 0.001% like Nathan Latka's podcast.

And sponsors might still not be interested in investing their money in your show.

"At the end of the day, people have to understand podcasting is not a business. You can't generate revenue immediately, you are overly dependent on the platform and need to keep producing content on a weekly basis, and if you decide to stop podcasting for 3 months you might lose all your listeners as they will fill the gap by finding similar content elsewhere."

If your project doesn't generate revenue, and more importantly, isn't profitable... then you don't have a business.

A virtual summit solves those problems while keeping all the benefits of podcasting.

It's important to have clear opening and closing summit dates, so attendees don't expect the event to last forever. And more importantly, you can sell summit recordings and include bonuses to generate revenue from your first series of interviews.

And if you are already thinking about launching a podcast, why not launch an improved version and get paid to do it since you are already interviewing experts?

You will be able to monetize your content, upsell your courses or masterminds, and also partner with other experts to launch products together. That's a hell of a lot better than a podcast with no income, right?

5. Speaking & Business Opportunities

By positioning yourself next to experts who regularly get invited to speak (and that's probably how you also found them), you will also get opportunities to be on stage.

When I hosted the Millennial Success Summit, I received 13 speaking invitations and several of them came from France, England, and Malaysia. One of those opportunities transformed into a 6-figure partnership for a future business.

The Airbnb Mastery Summit helped my Co-Founder get featured on national television as well as secure a speaking opportunity at a wealth conference where Pitbull, Anthony Robbins, and Magic Johnson were also presenting.

The cream of the cream was when **Netflix reached out and asked us to host** their new short-term rental shows.

Unfortunately that TV show never launched, but the opportunity presented itself because we were seen everywhere on social media within our industry during the month we launched.

After hosting the Crypto Virtual Summit, Amateo Ra was offered a position as lead marketing director of a Top 100 ICO company.

After a couple months, the company merged with another blockchain business started by Garrett Camp, Co-Founder of Uber. Amateo ascended to a more prominent role and is now the marketing anchor for two big blockchain companies.

6. Launch a Product

A virtual summit can be an amazing rocket fuel to launch a high-end product such as a retreat, mastermind or course.

Chandler Bolt already had a $2,000 course teaching aspiring authors how to write and publish a best-selling book on Amazon. He realized the leap from cold traffic to buying customers might be too big for his high-end packages.

So he built a *virtual summit* teaching the principles of self-publishing to familiarize his customers with his work in order to convert attendees into potential buyers.

After spending a couple days listening to Chandler and the experts he interviewed, they became more likely to buy since a relationship based on trust has been built with his new audience.

For the customers who weren't interested in the $2,000 package, Chandler sold hundreds of summit recordings to customers who only wanted to invest a few hundred dollars.

He went from 6,000 to over 30,000 emails by the time his summit ended. He is now on track to make 8 figures with his self-publishing company.

7. Learn From Experts

This was my #1 reason behind hosting my first summit.

I was still a little bit lost after launching my live event and I thought it would be great if to learn directly from entrepreneurs who were doing what I was interested in.

I was interested in building an online business but I didn't know where to start or what kind of business I wanted to launch.

Here's what I did: I gathered 35 entrepreneurs under age 35 who were generating at least 6 figures so I could brainpick experts from all those different industries ranging from Instagram, Ecommerce, branding, coaching, live streaming, book selling, and media, among other topics.

And I was able to talk with industry experts such as Jordan Harbinger (Art of Charm), Nicholas Kusmich (runs FB ads for Tony Robbins), and Nathan Chan (CEO of Foundr Magazine) who all ran multiple 7-figure companies.

I knew that if I wanted 1-on-1 time with them, it would cost me $5,000 per hour. BUT, under the frame of interviewing them on a virtual summit, I was able to talk to them for free and access their value while recording an episode for my summit. Win-win.

So I treated those interviews as if they were 1-hour VIP sessions with experts from 35 different industries. This allowed me to gain more insight into their different industries that I was interested in diving into.

That was the biggest goal for me: *getting access to & learning from the very best of each industry.*

And if the content I created was beneficial for the people who were watching my conversation to the point they wanted to purchase the videos (which of course it was), it was another win for me.

After hosting my virtual summit, friends kept asking me how I created those platforms. And that's how this book came to be.

WHY NOW IS THE BEST TIME

If you're serious about growing your business so you can earn respect and make more money, build your business, work less, or have the option to quit your job, this is the obvious next step.

I know what you're probably thinking: "But who am I to host a summit and interview experts?

If anyone had these excuses, it was me. I had just dropped out of college and was confused about the next steps to take in my life.

Heck. English isn't my first language. Not even my second one.

I had all the excuses in the world. But I also had nothing to lose.

So I just went ahead and did it despite the fear and limiting beliefs. And it paid off.

I was just 20 years old when I launched my first summit, which brought in tens of thousands of dollars in a few short months. It then led me to launch **multiple 6-figure businesses** with incredible business partners.

In this book I'm giving you the keys to my *step-by-step summit launch formula*, so you can start enjoying the same benefits that I discovered. It's the exact blueprint my virtual summit agency uses to launch dozens of summits in dozens of industries.

I've tested, tweaked, and perfected this formula.

If you follow what I'm about to lay out, **I guarantee that your virtual summit will become successful.** If you follow the proven formula in this book and take action, you will be able to launch a summit that will systematically grow your tribe, influence, and revenue.

No matter what objection you come up with, I can show you how to launch your summit and make passive income each and every month.

If you want to do it later, you can put this book down right now.

But if you want to get started and have a win under your belt that's going to make you feel confident in your ability to succeed, *start NOW*.

Chapter 3: Virtual Summit Myths Debunked

In this section you are going to learn:

- How to use shortcomings to your advantage
- Why the time and money input *isn't what you think*
- How virtual summits can be harnessed for *any industry*

When it comes to launching a virtual summit, a lot of people get deep in their heads and end up doubting themselves.

It's a big hurdle to overcome the self-doubt and believe in yourself enough to actually want to launch an event and DO it.

Hosting an event is a big confidence booster, but a mindset plagued with doubt is something that most entrepreneurs struggle with. Even the best ones.

You may question yourself with thoughts like, "Is what I offer going to be any good? Are people going to want to attend my event? Are people going to make fun of me? Is the going to profit? Am I going to make a fool of myself putting myself out there?"

These are all internal struggles that you have to get over, and it will be an ongoing battle throughout the process of launching your new venture, but you can overcome this kind of thinking.

In the previous chapter, I broke down all the ways a virtual summit can grow your business, make you more money, build your influence, and grow your tribe.

Now I want to hone in on the mental side of the business because that's arguably the most important part.

With my first virtual summit, although the end results were AMAZING, I still experienced the same doubts, fears, and insecurities others face. I didn't know if my event would be a success or a complete flop.

In fact, I was so lost and distressed that I surrendered to a *Fuck it* mentality.

"Fuck it. No matter how shitty my summit is going to be, I'm going to finish it and release it to the world. It might not be as great as I wanted it to be, but at least it'll be done".

The huge win for you is that you won't have to guess any step of the process like I did, which is the biggest element of doubt. So let's dive into the **7 limiting beliefs** when it comes to hosting a virtual summit.

1. I'm Not an Expert

"Who am I to ask questions to the speakers?

I don't know everything about the industry!

I don't want to look dumb during the interview...

The great thing about hosting a virtual summit is that **you don't have to be an expert.**

The spotlight will be cast on the speaker, and if you prepare 6-10 questions, you won't need to talk much more since attendees are there to listen to the speaker's answer. Not yours.

It's all about the packaging and the way you give the information. The more personal touch you give it, the better people will connect with your message.

In fact, **it can even be an advantage to not know much about a certain aspect of your industry.** This will make you a better and relatable interviewer (if you prepare your questions well) compared to an industry expert host who would assume certain pieces of information are common knowledge— leaving attendees confused. Use your objectivity to your advantage.

Your role as an interviewer is to make sure that the vast majority of attendees understand the principles your speakers are sharing. As long as you add value, it doesn't matter who you are, and you don't have to be an expert to add value. You just have to pull it out of others.

If you don't understand something very well, you can politely interrupt and ask the speaker to elaborate if you think your attendees would also benefit from it. Audience members might be thinking the same thing you are.

Do your research on the industry and speakers but don't sweat over sounding dumb because the speaker you are interviewing has spent years, if not decades, working in that specific field.

Everyone has to start somewhere, and you can help accelerate the learning curve by asking inquisitive questions.

2. **It's Too Expensive**

Virtual summits can actually be really cheap to launch depending on how much you are willing to do yourself.

I've seen summits costing over $75,000 and others launching for less than $1,000. The first summit I launched cost me less than $700 and generated over $10,000 in sales.

One of our agency-unique methodologies is that 100% of all the summits we launch are self-funded through sponsorship.

We never spent money from our own pocket since we're always looking for strategic partners to cover summit tech and marketing costs.

I will teach more in depth **in Chapter 12** with the techniques that we used to raise over $100,000 in sponsorships so that you can **be profitable before your event even starts**.

3. **It Takes a Lot of Time**

Summits can be launched fairly quickly if you already have the connections and messaging nailed down. Even if you don't, you'll have my entire system in this book which will save you *so much time.*

Interviews are usually what takes the most time (web design is a close second). The key is to map out your summit schedule and follow it to make sure you aren't overwhelmed or stressed out by the time you hit your deadline.

My summits take 90 days on average to launch, but if you need more time, take as much as you need to hit your goal. For reference, my first event took me 76 days to launch.

You can also hire agencies or teams to build your virtual summit platform so that you only have to focus on getting speakers onboarded and can move faster and more efficiently.

My virtual summit agency clients are typically 6 to 7-figure entrepreneurs and tribe leaders who want to build a high-conversion lead gen platform, but don't have the time to go through a book or a course to do it themselves. Time is money.

Having a team of experienced designers, marketing strategists, and copywriters, **who understand exactly what needs to be done** and when, saves them tremendous amounts of time and money.

4. I Don't Have a Network or Know Any Speakers

Sure, it's always a great time saver to know some industry leaders before starting a summit, but it also isn't a problem if you don't have an established network (yet)!

I only knew 10% of the speakers on my first summit, and 100% of the speakers on the Crypto Virtual Summit were reached *cold*. Keep in mind that most of our speakers on the crypto summit were either high-level executives or CEOs of billion-dollar companies— you will be surprised by how simple it can be to get a YES from A-type speakers.

So how did we do it?

We approached speakers one by one. Each speaker we booked led to getting a bigger one. I'll share the strategies you can use to find anyone's personal email and how to invite them to be a summit speaker in Chapter 10.

5. I Love the Idea, But it's Not Applicable in My Industry

If there's an existing audience or live event, there's a need that can be served online. Really.

There have been some really niched-down summits that work well, such as the Harp Virtual Summit, Social Man Summit, Crohn's Disease & Colitis Summit, BBQ Summit, Crypto Summit... you get the idea.

There are tons of summits with themes not related to business or making money that are widely successful. If you're still wondering how to find your profitable summit theme, we will explore that together in Chapter 6.

6. I Don't Know Where To Start

When I built my first summit, I had no idea what I was jumping into. I had no experience in building online businesses, nor did I have much savings left in my bank account after hosting my live event.

And I did something nobody should do in such a short amount of time: I built the entire summit infrastructure and launched a virtual summit in 76 days.

Since I didn't have much money, I did everything myself and felt rushed to launch as soon as I could. I built the website and inner pages, wrote the copy for the landing page and email sequences, reached out to speakers and sponsors, edited the videos, and even replied to all the customer service emails before, during, and after the event.

I wouldn't recommend this experience to anyone since it took me literally weeks to recover from the accumulated fatigue and stress— mainly because I spent a lot of time figuring things out on my own.

But this experience allowed me to gain a deep understanding of *each moving piece* that needs to be assembled in order to launch a successful and profitable virtual summit. I refined my system and tools over the years— and finally **created a system that anyone can follow** to build a successful event.

If you are lost during the process, you can go back to this book or email me directly at eric@leadnextgen.com if you have any questions. Seriously.

This book is designed to guide you every step of the way as I was really unsatisfied with the quality of the content I saw online (and also because my friends keeps asking me how they could launch a summit).

7. My Summit Needs to be Perfect

Many people are fixated on the thought that that ONE event is going to change everything. There's a chance it might, but once you go through this process, I promise you'll see how easy it is to do again and again... and with each round you'll create an even better summit.

Just taking that pressure off will make the writing process a lot easier.

The thing that really helped me launch my first book was having low expectations. I know that seems strange to say, but it's true. But I don't mean this all-around. The biggest mistake people make with their first summit is having super high expectations, so they never launch because they're so scared that it might fail. They never want to release it because it seems like such a scary thing.

For me, I said: "Oh, I'm going to release my 20+ interviews and see what comes out of it." That took a lot of the pressure off and made it a much more enjoyable process. And you have in your hands the best possible tool to host an event that you can be truly proud of.

Chapter 4: The Proof

In this section you are going to learn:

- What tools I enabled to achieve consistent summit success
- How recent, real-life examples can be directly applied to your venture
- How these methods work across any industry or topic

If you're still reading this book, it should be pretty obvious that **hosting a virtual summit is something you need to do to grow your business**. Before I go into the nitty gritty details, I want to show you some proof that what I'm about to teach you *works*.

To do that, I'll give you a couple of success stories from people who followed the same exact system that I'll be teaching you in this book.

Crypto Virtual Summit

Amateo is known as one of the most talented and effective intuitive mentors in the consciousness, coaching, and emergent technology space. He came across bitcoin in 2013 and saw the surge of fake information when bitcoin hit 10K in late 2017.

Having spent hundreds of hours researching cryptocurrency, invested thousands of his own money, and gathered a huge community asking him for more information, he decided to create a crypto guide for his audience.

But Amateo had a challenge. Despite its win-win nature, cryptocurrency and blockchain technologies had a mixed reputation.

The crypto world is known as a hotbed for get-rich-quick schemes, and Amateo knew that there was a bigger opportunity in this model than people realized— if he could just get the message out.

→ HE DECIDED TO HOST A VIRTUAL SUMMIT TO SET THE RECORD STRAIGHT ON HIS INDUSTRY.

Because of the mixed reputation of cryptocurrencies, the technology side has been widely ignored. Amateo realized a summit was the best way to elevate the conversation for newcomers and crypto enthusiasts so the entire industry could benefit from more informed investors.

As a busy business owner, Amateo knew the message he wanted to share but struggled to find the time and experience to make it happen. So he reached out to our agency and we started working together.

Before the summit, Amateo had trouble standing out as a key leader in his field. He didn't have any direct contact with blockchain founders or companies, nor did he have an established brand within the blockchain industry.

→ THE SUMMIT ALLOWED AMATEO TO CONNECT AND INTERVIEW HIS DREAM SPEAKERS: TOP 100 ICO COMPANY FOUNDERS AND CEOS.

Not only was he able to connect with industry leaders he has been following for years, but Amateo also partnered and raised well over $75,000 in sponsorships through the Crypto Virtual Summit brand.

This summit was a _wild success_ and gathered over 4,000 attendees from 17 countries. Attendees no longer had to paid thousands of dollars and spend 3 days in a conference room just to access the latest information from top speakers.

The event generated close to **$70,000 in profit.**

Because it's accessible, clear, and honest, Crypto Virtual Summit is paving the way to help non-industry individuals appreciate blockchain technologies while learning how to invest wisely.

As he'd hoped, Amateo became mentioned on high profile blockchain companies' social media and several other influential crypto media sites, while attendees gave him powerful and positive feedback on his event.

The unexpected crown jewel was getting hired as Lead Marketing Director for a company that went public shortly afterwards. This company grew to over 50 members and also invested by Garrett Camp, the Co-founder of Uber.

Thanks to the summit, Amateo is getting hands-on experience in a blockchain company that has promising growth and technology.

Airbnb Mastery Summit

After spending 4 years selling properties in New Jersey, Eric D. Moeller decided to move to San Diego in 2017 to create a short-term rental business and manage properties across the United States through Airbnb.

By running the math, he saw that managing short-term rentals could have an ROI up to 130% compared to renting apartments on yearly contracts.

Through perfecting his own short term rental system, Eric saw the information gap in the industry and wanted to position himself as the go-to Airbnb guy.

After failing to launch his own course and personal brand, he felt frustrated that his email list, webinars, and web traffic were not performing the way he wanted. With an email list of less than 100, he wanted to launch an online event.

→ ERIC KNEW A VIRTUAL SUMMIT WOULD ELEVATE HIS STATUS BUT ALSO KNEW HE COULDN'T DO IT ALONE.

This is how Eric partnered with our agency, and we helped him launch a virtual summit teaching how to build a business on Airbnb.

Thanks to the unique appeal of virtual summits (*Online, Free, Easy to Access*), Eric was able to connect with mentors, influencers, and icons he's been following since his debut in the real estate world.

We raised close to $25,000 in sponsorships and allocated half of those funds for our Facebook Ads campaign.

The summit generated over **$85,000** in revenue and gathered over 8,500 attendees.

One of our Facebook Live clips went semi-viral: gathering at least 21,000 organic views, 900 comments & 120k in reach.

All the attention was nice, but ultimately, Eric's main goal was to grow his business.

And that's exactly what happened naturally. Since he put himself out there and is now the authority leader, opportunities have been coming out of the woodwork. Attendees are reaching out wanting to work with him.

→ SOME SPEAKERS BECAME STRATEGIC PARTNERS AS ERIC LEVERAGED HIS POSITION AS A SUMMIT HOST TO ADD VALUE AND CREATE $3 MILLION WORTH OF PARTNERSHIPS.

The virtual summit immediately propelled Eric's brand to the next level. Another big focus was getting speaking engagements to appear in front of his ideal audience. By the time the summit launched, Eric had already set up interviews on national TV and numerous real estate podcast invites.

Only a few weeks after the summit ended, he received invitations from major associations, conferences, and other groups. Notably, one of Eric's invites was to speak and sell on stage at Real Estate Wealth Expo— Los Angeles. Netflix also reached out to us about potentially Co-Creating a TV show.

→ MORE IMPORTANTLY, THE AIRBNB MASTERY SUMMIT HELPED ERIC COMMAND RESPECT AND AUTHORITY IN THE SHORT-TERM RENTAL SPACE.

Once this authority is established, you can basically take it whatever direction you like.

Eric was able to circle back to his original plan and launch his "Co-Host Mastery" online course. The summit re-launch gathered over 10,000 attendees as well.

These are just a few of the *many* success stories from people just like you who have used the system you're about to learn.

Our agency currently helps launch at least 1 summit per month. All of our clients have become authority leaders and are making passive income from the summits we've executed.

Each of them are experiencing amazing results, and you can too if you commit to following the strategies in this book.

On a deeper level, it was even more life-changing because so many of these people had been frustrated all their lives but didn't know how to take the first step to become financially free. This might even sound familiar to you as well.

Hosting an online event is that stepping stone. Maybe you want to be a public speaker, a coach, or an entrepreneur. Hosting a conference and getting paid to learn is *the first step* toward this transformation.

Having a platform that generates leads, creates authority, and generates revenue changes the game.

From a personal perspective, I felt incredibly fulfilled getting so much love for distributing great content. Everyone around me thought I was a genius for creating masterclasses in under-served industries.

In the upcoming chapters I will lay out the foundation for **being a successful summit host even if you've never interviewed anyone before in your life**.

I will also provide a **proven system for marketing so your event is guaranteed to be successful** when you launch.

The following chapters might be a little less story-focused at times because I'll be teaching the step-by-step process in detail... holding nothing back.

Continue reading all the way to the end. I promise it will all be worth it.

But first, you'll need to step into the mindset of a successful virtual host by avoiding common mistakes most people make.

Chapter 5: 6 Mistakes Most Summit Hosts Make

In this section you are going to learn:

- How your best intentions might be sabotaging your success and reputation
- Why free offers actually earn you *more money*
- How you may be bypassing key leads

---

1. Forcing Your Summit Speakers to Promote

This is the *#1 mistake* summit hosts make when they invite speakers on their summit. **It's the best way to ruin your reputation and destroy a relationship before it even begins.**

It's one thing to encourage a speaker to promote but forcing them is a different story. You need to come from a place of abundance.

Yes of course, generally speaking, the speakers' email list would be the most receptive audience to attend that event since they already know someone speaking on it.

But *nobody is entitled to anyone's community.*

A lot of speakers decline to be on a virtual summit but agree to get interviewed on a podcast even if the time commitment is relatively the same. You can guess why.

They know that most summit hosts are going to ask them to promote it, and they save the drama by saying no— even if it might be beneficial for their brand.

If you are wondering how to get attendees to your event without relying on your speaker's network, we'll cover it in *Chapter 12*.

2. Hosting a Summit Nobody Wants

A great idea for you might not be one to the rest of the world. The market is never wrong and it's our responsibility as entrepreneurs to do the research before launching any project.

One of my friends wanted to launch a virtual summit on Human Resources by interviewing Fortune 500 companies on how to manage employees effectively.

Although there's a clear need for startups and medium size companies to learn how to navigate communication with their employees, there wasn't a clear customer avatar and acquisition strategy for the summit.

After 9 months of hard work, only a few hundred attendees signed up, despite getting speakers from Facebook, Google, Amazon, Airbnb, and Apple.

The summit had a lot of potential but his messaging and summit outcomes were unclear. If the host is confused, so will customers. And confused customer never buys.

A clear summit theme is the foundation of your summit's success. If you build a house on unstable ground you'll end up with a crumbling house, no matter how great your materials are.

In *Chapter 6,* you will learn how to find your profitable summit theme. A properly defined summit will pull your target audience like a powerful magnet and ensure great profitability. You will save months of work and hardships by having clear foundations.

3. Bad Design and Complicated Tech Setup

Let's say you have the best summit theme idea, an incredible lineup of speakers, and a significant marketing budget.

You are ready to pull the trigger but the website crashes. It doesn't matter how great your speakers are if your summit infrastructure isn't set up the right way.

What if your servers or payment processor suddenly stopped working in the middle of your launch? You can also potentially lose over $100,000 in sales by choosing the wrong shopping cart or hosting platform. This has actually happened countless times and has destroyed many business launches.

It's also important to determine which things are necessities and which are optional for your summit launch.

The rule of thumb is to keep it simple on your first summit, follow the instructions from proven systems that have been tested over and over again, and gradually modify your pages once you've built a proven track record.

In *Chapter 11*, you are going to have a list of all the essential features that constitute an attractive landing page to *book your dream speakers*. We'll also give you the blueprint to build your inner-pages and funnels for maximum conversion rates.

4. Paying Summit > Free Summit

There are different school of thoughts on whether a summit should be free or paid.

Some summits make their attendees pay an entrance fee before the summit starts. (I am not talking about upsell offers here, but about paying an entrance fee to attend the summit.)

I personally think it's a terrible strategy that goes against the benefits of hosting a virtual summit.

In that scenario, customers pre-pay to have access to interviews and would need to buy the all-access pass to own the recordings.

If your virtual summit goal is to create brand exposure, build credibility, grow a large email list, and generate high potential revenue, it's strongly encouraged that you focus on having the largest amount of people register and converting those attendees into buying customers.

By making your attendees pay a fee to attend your online conference, you are drastically decreasing the amount of emails you can capture on your landing page.

Attendees are also less likely to share the summit to their friends, and sponsors/speakers are less likely to partake because your reach will be less attractive than a free summit.

In most cases, and for most businesses, **a free summit is the way to go**.

It's a far more powerful way to reach a wide audience, build trust and loyalty, and expand your potential. Don't worry, just because it's free doesn't mean you won't be making money.

You are also more likely to make less money by hosting a paid summit (which might sound counter-intuitive). Here are some real numbers from Paid vs. Free Summit in similar niches (in this example, the fitness market).

Free Summit
Facebook Ads Budget: $13,000
Paid traffic Results: 8,835 (emails)
All-Access Pass: 4.3% x $247 = $112,860

Paid Summit
Facebook Marketing Budget: $15,000
Paid Traffic Results: 2239 emails
2,239 attendees x $7 = $15,673
130 customers (4.1% of attendees) x $247 = $28,158
Total in sales: $43,831

See? Pretty interesting, right?
Don't step over long-term dollars chasing short-term pennies.

5. Not Having Summit Goals

Goal-setting is an <u>absolute must</u> for people who want to succeed, find their true purpose, and create joy in their lives.

Without clear goals, you will not have a clear direction on where you're heading in your life. When you know your life purpose, determine your vision, convert your desires into achievable goals and then act on them, you're virtually guaranteed success.

After decades of research into how the human brain works, **scientists now know that for our brains to figure out how to get what we want, we must first decide what we want.**

Once we lock in our desires through goal-setting, our mind can step in to help make our dreams a reality.

When there isn't any criteria for measurement and it's simply something you want, we call it a wish, a preference, or just a good idea— but it doesn't register in the mind as a goal.

What is a SMART Goal?

No matter what you call your goals, they must be *specific and measurable*. One of the best methods of goal-setting is setting SMART Goals.

Ensure that your goals are *Specific, Measurable, Attainable, Relevant, and Time-bounded*. You have a bigger chance of achieving SMART goals than those that are vague and too broad or don't have a specific target date for completion.

S- Specific
When goal-setting, your goal must be very clear and defined not only to you but to others as well. It should be precise, detailed, and capable of answering questions instead of creating more.

M- Measurable
Include dates, exact financial numbers, and amounts in your goal. Your goal shouldn't be "Make more money", it should state a specific amount, by a specific time. More like, "I will make $10,000 extra dollars by January 1st, 2019". If the goal is broken down into steps, each step must be measurable as well.

A- Attainable
Your goal must be achievable. You should be able to accomplish it within the constraints of time, money, and environment, as well as your skills, abilities and other important factors. However, I do recommend you set a couple goals for yourself that I call "breakthrough goals" or a goal that is really going to push you to attain.

R- Realistic
Goals should be in line with the direction that you're heading in life. Keep your goals in line with your true purpose. Don't waste time with unrealistic goals.

T- Time-Bounded

Always set specific deadlines for the completion of your goal. Creating a target date of completion creates accountability and gives you more motivation. If you don't achieve your goal by your specific date that's ok, just adjust and keep moving forward. Always set a date for your goals.

6. Not Finishing Strong

This is where most summits *waste the majority of their untapped potential.*

After working over 3 months on a tremendous project and building a strong community of ideal clients and connections, people also have content, leverage, and a platform that allows anyone to partner with established brands and companies.

And most do nothing about it. They stop engaging with their community on social media and/or emails.

Following up and finishing strong by looking for new partnerships, re-launching your summit, and repurposing your content into attractive lead magnet tools can be the *It* factor to differentiate yourself from your competition.

We'll go over that in Chapter 14.

Chapter 6: How To Pick Your Virtual Summit Theme

In this section you are going to learn:

- How to find your summit theme when you feel lost
- How to make sure your passion also <u>pays</u>
- How to save yourself time and money with the right research

---

In this chapter, we'll explore how to find your perfect summit theme then take that information to research how profitable and marketable you summit can become.

Maybe you have a subject or topic but need some help clarifying what you want the focus of your event.

I know that this can seem a little intimidating, but it will help you even if you don't have the slightest idea (especially if you don't have a business, this chapter will be great for you).

There's a big difference between hosting a simple summit and having a summit that drives a lot of attention, sales, and attendees.

You discovered in Chapter 2 why a summit can help you in your business and life. This chapter will help you define what your summit will be about.

And I created a system on how to find your "what" during my gap year between high school and college.

After watching countless soul-searching movies, I decided to travel around the world to 'find myself'. Fast forwards 9 months later, I was still lost as fuck.

My last destination was Japan where I had one of the most memorable evenings at a casual Japanese dinner organized by mom's friends. She invited to come along to a meal with several of her classmates

I asked where they all went to school.

"We all met Harvard Business School and came back to Japan after we graduated."

I replied with a simple "Ah".

18-year-old me instantly felt intimidated. Not wanting to say anything stupid, I sat down and carefully listened to the adults talking.

After 10 minutes of sitting at the corner of the table, one of the classmates asked me what I wanted to do when I grew up.

"I've been trying to find an answer for the past year but couldn't find anything," I said.

"I thought that traveling around the world would help me find my passion or at least find myself. But I am still as lost as when I first started my journey."

"What have you tried to find what you wanted to do?" he asked

I took a second to think about it. "I asked people what they liked and how they found their passion. But most of their answers was something along the lines of 'pure luck' or "it was a random discovery', which didn't help me much."

Then I asked him if he had any advice to give me about finding my passion but also being able to live off it.

This is when he taught me the Japanese concept for happiness and search for meaning called Ikigai (pronounce ee-kee-guy).

He shared that for many people, striving to find their purpose in life can resemble a similar winding quest, filled with many twists and wrong turns.

Some blindly follow passions that aren't based in reality, then wind up feeling discouraged when their dreams don't materialize. Others resign themselves to careers that bring them money and status, but aren't fulfilling. In both cases, over time, their sense of purpose can begin to fade.

So What is Ikigai?

It roughly means the "thing that you live for" or "the reason for which you get up in the morning". In a nutshell, Ikigai encompasses the idea that happiness in life is about more than money or a fancy job title.

Ikigai has a few essential qualities that separate it from the "follow your passion" truism as we conceive of it in Western culture:

- **It's challenging.** Your Ikigai should lead to mastery and growth. It won't always be easy and hard work is expected.

- **It's your choice.** You feel a certain degree of autonomy and freedom pursuing your Ikigai. It involves a commitment of time and belief, perhaps to a particular cause, skill, trade, or group of people.

- **It boosts your well-being.** Ikigai is associated with positive relationships and good health.

- **It gives you more energy** than it takes away.

But it's important to understand that figuring out your Ikigai doesn't happen overnight. Rather than being something that you magically discover, your purpose unfolds and will evolve over time.

That's not an excuse to sit back and expect your Ikigai to present itself. Finding it requires a willingness for deep self-exploration and experimentation, and there are ways to work on that.

Thoughtful reflection combined with action-taking can help you to uncover how your values, strengths, and skills can be brought to the forefront to help you find more meaning in your life and career—and the balance of Ikigai.

Not every moment of every day will be blissful. Keep in mind that even as you pursue your sense of purpose, it won't always be easy or even enjoyable. Regardless of the changes you've made in your career or life, you'll likely still have to make tradeoffs and compromises from time to time.

If you're connected with your sense of purpose most of the time, though, you'll be more resilient and keep bad days in perspective.

"Okay Eric, this is great, but what does that have to do with my virtual summit?"

Here's why.

The perfect theme will sit at the intersection between:

1. **Knowing What You Love & Are Good At (Summit Theme)**
2. **Giving What the World Needs (Marketing To The Right People)**
3. **Getting Paid for That Service or Product (Offer)**

How to Find Your Summit Theme When You Are Lost

Too many of us believe in a magical thing called 'passion'. "If only I could find my passion", we cry, "Finding my passion would make me happy."

Passion is very real and extremely powerful. But almost everything people believe about finding it is wrong. And it's completely normal if you don't have something you are deeply passionate about. Most people die without ever really living.

Rule 1: Passion Comes from Success

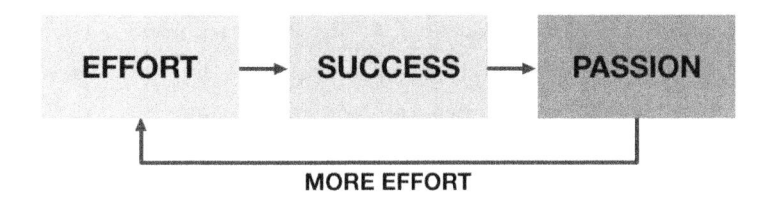

EFFORT → SUCCESS → PASSION

MORE EFFORT

All of our emotions exist for good reason. We feel hunger to ensure we don't starve. We feel full to ensure we don't burst. And we feel passion to ensure we concentrate our efforts on things that reward us the most.

Imagine starting a cooking class. You find it easy. You realize you're getting better than others, and fast. That rising excitement you feel is your passion, and that passion makes you come back for more, improve your skills, and compound your strengths.

The enemy of passion is frustration. If you constantly struggle with something, you'll never become passionate about it. You learn to avoid it entirely, which guarantees that you never improve.

```
EFFORT → FRUSTRATION
     ↑_____|
       LESS EFFORT
```

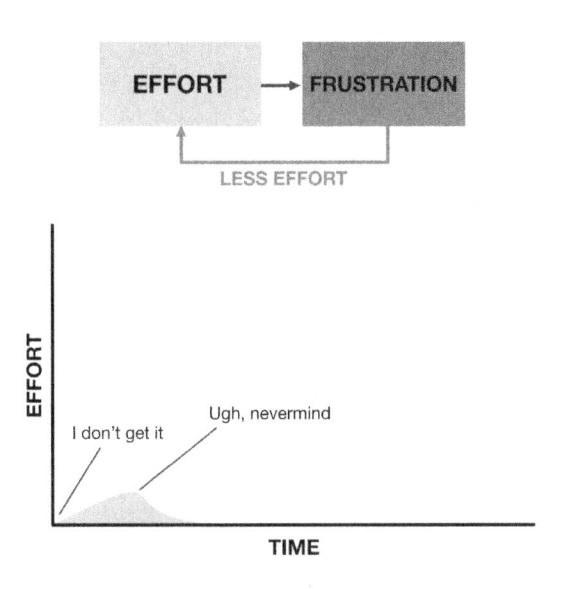

[Graph: Effort vs Time, showing a small bump labeled "I don't get it" rising and "Ugh, nevermind" falling]

Most people get this backwards. They think we discover our passion, and that makes us good at something. It's actually finding that you're good which comes first. Passion comes from success.

"What if I Don't Know What I'm Passionate About?"

Rule 2: Passion can be Created

Most successful people in life generally didn't pick their passion off a shelf.

In fact, many of the world's most successful people dropped out of education entirely. Not because they were stupid, but because they found other areas where they were more skilled that education did not recognize.
They created their own passions. Only a tiny fraction of people can expect to excel in the narrow subjects that childhood or formal education primes us for.

And competition in that space is basically 'everybody in the world who went to school', which doesn't help our chances.

But if you look outside of that space, you'll find less competition, and more options. And this is how you tip the odds of finding a passion in your favour. That's your unfair advantage.

The key is picking something you are the most curious about and take action. The confusion will disappear.

Exercise (Grab a Pen)

Give yourself at least 3 full minutes for each question. Don't stop writing during that time. The goal is to generate as many answers as possible even if they might sound weird.

You can also grab your printable worksheet with advanced instructions & details on **leadnextgen.com/book-bonus**

Here are some questions to help you find your summit theme:

1. List the things you have a strong interest in. Can you spend 500+ hours learning about it?
2. What do you wish you could become better at? And why?
3. List the names of 30 people you admire (fictional or real):
   a) What industry are they in?
   b) What traits do you admire?
   c) Is it something that can be taught?
4. If you could learn anything, what would it be?
5. Is there a personal mission you have, or something you want to share with the world?
6. What did you used to love as a kid but gave up growing up because of lack of time, money, and/or energy?
7. If money wasn't an issue, what would you spend your time doing?

Ask yourself what you want to be known for. A successful summit will open doors and opportunities as thousands of potential attendees and companies perceive you as the established leader.

Additional Exercise Resources

If the timed free-writing exercise was a challenge for you, there are always four categories that sell really well. These niches attract the most attention and if these topics interest you, choose one and go deeper into one of these categories:

1. Diet and Fitness
2. Relationships
3. Time Management or Stress Management
4. How to Make More Money

a) Research Top Podcasts in Different Niches

You can generate tons of great summit idea by navigating through Itunes' podcast list— like business, education, health, or any relevant theme in your industry.

I would suggest not only looking at the best rated podcasts but also writing down their most popular episodes name and speaker. Each podcast episode can serve as potential topic on your summit. The podcast hosts has already done part of the market research by openly sharing their metrics on the platform.

b) Popular Classes Online

Go to google and search for courses in your industry such as "list-building course or "Instagram course"

A lot of platforms share how many courses they've sold which is a good indicator whether there's a high demand for that type of content.

- Udemy.com
- Coursera.org
- Lynda.com
- Creativelive.com
- Skillshare.com

c) Amazon Books

Take a look at the bestseller lists for books, or type in your keywords and see what comes up. Look for the most popular items or books— the ones with a lot of reviews. And read the reviews, too! You can see what people are looking for in their own words.

What you are trying to do during the refinement phase is solve a pain point that your potential readers have.

- Branch out to other categories to see if there is a hole in the market.
- Look at the books that are selling and see what they have inside.
- Take a look at the book description and the comments to see what people are saying.

By the end of this exercise, you should have a ton of ideas about different topics that you could do a summit on. But remember not all of these ideas are GOOD ideas— the point is to get creative and come up with more ideas, then you can validate the idea and choose the best one later.

Don't get caught up with whether or not you have the perfect topic for your book. You can always refine and narrow it even more as you write; the important thing is to start writing. In the next chapter, you will find out just how simple it is to research your industry.

Chapter 7: Does the Market Need Your Summit?

In this section you are going to learn:

- How to follow the right examples
- How to avoid an unsuccessful summit
- How to well-defined your customer with a clear avatar

The best way to find out if there's high demand for your summit is to research the successful in-person events in your industry. It's important that you put a good amount into this phase in order to avoid the risk of **hosting a summit that appeals to nobody**.

This is one of the biggest mistakes people make, and it's crucial that you don't fall into this group. If you move forward with crafting a product that people *don't want, need, or understand*, you're costing yourself time, money, and reputation. Not to mention, the rapid rise of virtual summits means that this setback could cause you to miss out on key topics because someone else tackled them while you were focused on an unsuccessful one. Don't let this be you.

Luckily, there are some ways to avoid it if you follow these steps.

Accelerate your learning curve by taking the best and leaving the rest.

7.1 Find Examples of Other Summits

Google "your niche + summit" such as "crypto virtual summit" or "self-publishing summit"

Repeat the search with similar search terms such as:

- Your niche + event
- Your niche + online summit
- Your niche + conference

This is your checklist to organize your research so you can model what works on your own summit. I recommend doing this exercise on at least 3 different events.

1) What is the name of their summit?
2) How many speakers does the summit have?
3) What is their summit theme?
4) How do they monetize their event (sponsors, tickets, upsell, retreat)?
5) What are the top 3 things that made their website great?
6) Do they have a Facebook community? If so, what makes their community great?
7) Did you subscribe to their email list?

7.2 Customer Avatar

Every successful business *needs* a clear customer avatar. No question.

Just take a look at the top players out there right now— whether you recognize it or not, what sets them apart and puts them at the top of their game is how well they know their audience and clients.

A huge part of your success depends on how clear you are with your target audience. It's not enough to have a general idea of who your customers might be. Defining the portrait of your ideal customer **is the most important exercise of any business**. *If you don't know what your customer wants, you can't give it to them.*

By defining a detailed customer avatar, you can know exactly the type of person you are trying to reach and what would make them want to buy your product, as well as what would potentially make them pass on a product. You can use this information to anticipate any reasons for refusal and craft an offer that captures their sale. This why the more specific you are, the better. It's crucial to do this exercise thoroughly, because *your Facebook Ads campaign will pull heavily from this exercise* as well.

Once you've defined your dream customer avatar, you want to **design the entire summit experience as if it was created for this one person alone**.

Curating their dream experience and making them truly excited about your product will **transform your customers into raving fans**. These raving fans are the ones who will constantly share your product to their friends and communities. They help carry out your marketing organically and expand your reach to their network who fits the same avatar and demographic.

They're also the ones who will engage with your community, answer others' questions, and participate in your survey because they are the ones who care the most. And the best way to attract raving fans is to understand their deepest pains and biggest dreams.

Now that you know how much you *need* this, here's how you do it:

A) Name Your Customer Avatar

B) Demographics
- Male or female?
- How old are they?
- Single, in a relationship, married?

- What is their ethnicity?
- Where do they live?
- What is their income?
- What industry are they in?
- How long have they been working?

C) Current Situation
- Are they happy with their current situation? If not, why?
- What prevents them from changing?
- What are they frustrated about?
- What is their biggest obstacle to get what they want?
- Which social media platform do they spend the most time on?

D) Goals & Aspirations
- What are their personal goals?
- What will happen to them if their current situation gets worse or doesn't change?
- How would that impact other people in their life (friends, family, business)?
- What do they Google to solve their problems/frustrations?
- What is their dream solution that they would be willing to pay almost anything for?
- How will their life become better because of your content/summit/product/service?
- What are the potential objections and hesitations they may have before purchasing?

E) Favorite Things (3 for each category)
- Magazine
- Podcast
- Youtube Channel
- Event/Retreat/Seminar
- Author
- Industry Leader

- Blog
- Facebook Community

All of this might seem like a lot of detail, and it is. But that's what makes it so valuable. Once you know everything about your customer, you can tap into exactly what they're looking for in a way that's mutually beneficial.

Chapter 8: Can You Get Paid For It? (Profitability & Offer)

In this section you are going to learn:

- How to create a summit offer that can't be refused
- How to identify the right industry leaders
- How to price for the perfect sale

After brainstorming several summit themes, researching your competition, and defining a clear customer avatar, you should now have all the information you need to launch a virtual summit.

The last piece of the puzzle is to make sure your summit can actually be **profitable.**

It can seem like a lot of work and expenses to cover, especially if you aren't tech savvy. But if you follow the instructions in this book, you'll end up saving thousands of dollars and generate revenue before you even launch your summit!

We were able to build a profitable summit because we knew other experts and industry leaders who already launched successful info-products but also because we had an offer rich in value through our all-access pass.

Creating a Value-Rich Offer

The trick is to hone in on exactly what your audience wants and needs to **put together an offer that they can't refuse.** A good way to do this is to include bonuses in your *All Access Pass* that are relevant and help people to apply the content from the summit.

A rule of thumb is to create bonuses that are actually more valuable than the recording itself. Once attendees learn that what you teach is valuable, they will want to know how they can implement it in their life or business.

For the Airbnb Mastery Summit, we shared strategies on how anyone could build a profitable Airbnb business in less than 90 days without owning a house. Once attendees learned what to do, they needed the *how* to do.

These bonuses included marketing templates for their listings, checklists for their houses, examples of contracts with landlords, and access to a community of other short-term rental entrepreneurs. Bonuses can include things like:

- Audio, slides or transcript download for each speaker session
- PDF Action Guides of the sessions
- A private community or mastermind
- Live Q&A sessions with you and speakers
- Offers from speakers, sponsors or partners
- Templates, swipe copy, checklists, cheat sheets, guides to download
- Ticket to LIVE event
- Special deals or discounts on related software or products
- Access to private Facebook community
- Special training with speakers and sponsors
- Quiz or personality tests

Depending on your industry, the pricing for an all-access pass can vary from $47 to $497. Clearly the difference is really big, which is why you must do the research on your competition and how much they price their events and products.

You always want to be **significantly cheaper and more valuable than your competition** so when your customer sees your offer, it becomes a no-brainer decision.

Something I always do on my summit is **reward fast-action takers** (buyers). They are usually the ones who are the most easy to work with because they tend to be the most emotionally invested in their problems and are willing to spend money to get a solution fast.

We usually have a special 15-minute discount price that comes out after someone signs up. For the Crypto Virtual Summit, our All-Access Pass during the summit was priced at $297 but we gave a 50% discount ($147) for people who wanted purchased the All-Access Pass immediately.

It looked like something like this:
1. 15-minute offer: $147
2. During event: $297
3. Post event: $497

You usually have **90% of your sales between the 15-minute offer and the post-event sales**. But you can generate a great amount of last-minute sales by following up with your customers after the summit ends.
That's how we generated an additional $5,000 minimum on the Airbnb Mastery Summit.

_____

Putting all the pieces together:
- Why You Want To Host A Summit
- Your Summit Goals
- Your Summit Demographic
- Your Summit Theme
- Your Offering

STOP:

Do NOT move to the next chapter unless you have done the previous exercises.

These next couple chapters may seem out of the blue, but when you actually go through this process, it is structured exactly as it should be.

So bear with me. All of this is going to make perfect sense.

Chapter 9: Creating a Summit Name and Hook

In this section you are going to learn:

- How to tap into the wants and needs of your audience
- How to select a name that sells
- How to communicate value to your audience

By this chapter, you should have a good idea of 3 things:
- Why you want to launch a virtual summit
- What your virtual summit is about
- Your offering and summit theme

Now that you have a clear purpose, demographic, and theme behind your virtual summit, the process for developing a name and hook should be a little easier.

How to Find a Summit Name

Crafting a good name is like putting together a puzzle. You need to see the picture on the puzzle box to know how to put it together.

When it comes to creating a title and subtitle for your book, most of you have all the pieces laid out in front of you but no picture to guide you.

The process I'm about to show you will help you see the big picture. I will help you whittle away all of the craziness in your brain until you get down to what actually matters: a summit title that appeals to your target audience and pulls them in.

1. Who is Your Audience?
Again, you must first think about who is the one person you could serve that would instantly gain value from what you are sharing. You need to be thoughtful about the specific person you can help more than anyone else.

You will want to be as narrow and specific as possible in answering this question.

As I said before, the more specific you get with your summit and your audience, the more you will help people.

Think "greater impact" instead of "greater reach".

2. What Will People Gain By Attending Your Summit?
The benefits are one of the main reasons people will attend your event. These benefits should be clear and concise.

List all the advantages that your summit will provide, and again, make them as specific as possible. It's okay to make bold claims — just make sure you deliver. People want things that will provide them benefits.

Example: The Airbnb Mastery Summit: Everything you need to know to start, grow, and scale a 6 figure short-term rental business in 6 months without buying a house.

This hook gives away how attendees are going to learn how to make more money at their job or business, spend less time doing things they hate, and have more time to live their life to the fullest — without exactly throwing this message in their faces.

3. Write 25 Summit Titles and Choose the Top 3

After asking yourself tough questions and getting the big picture, take a look at your book. Go ahead and write out the first 25 summit titles that come to your mind. Don't think. Just write.

The more you write, the more will come to mind. Don't hesitate to go big and bold.

Get to 25 and keep going past that if you can. Once you get to where you can't possibly write any more variations of titles, pick your top three.

Take those top three choices and get feedback from friends or post it on social media.

Chapter 10: Finding and Booking Your Dream Speakers

In this section you are going to learn:

- Why it's important to have influencers
- How to book your dream speakers
- What you need before reaching out to speakers
- After getting a "Yes", what's next?

10.1 Why Having Influencers Matters

Influencers play an important role in the creation and successful launch of your summit.

a) Quality Content
The best content doesn't always come from the most famous speakers, but it is always better to learn about a topic from an expert than someone who doesn't have much credentials or track record.

b) Promote Your Summit To More People
If you have a pre-established relationship with the influencer, they could potentially promote your summit to their audience. On the Airbnb Mastery Summit we interviewed Than Merrill, CEO of Fortune Builder, who owns one of the largest real estate education companies in the US. We grew a highly engaged and targeted email list by having him promote the summit to his highly curated RE community.

c) Anchor Strategy
Getting an influencer or A-type speaker on the summit creates immediate authority and trust within your summit. The attendees or potential speakers

might not know you, but if you manage to get the Michael Jordan of your niche, everyone else will want to associate their name and brand next to that thought leader. One famous speaker attracts other famous speakers. You will only need one.

I didn't have any established authority when I was building my first summit. The invitations I sent out were either rejected or ignored. But once I had Jordan Harbinger from the Art of Charm podcast, speakers started reaching out to me to become part of the summit.

d) Facebook Marketing Strategies
Even if a speaker decides they don't want to promote the summit to their email list, you can still target their audience on Facebook Ads.

It works even better if they have a big following on FB since the influencer's audience is more likely to be receptive to attend an event if they recognize someone they already trust.

By using this strategy, your conversion rate and cost per lead will become significantly lower.

10.2 Types of Influencers

a) A-Type Celebrities/Speakers (High Visibility)
They are the top .1% of your industry (Gary Vaynerchuk, Russell Brunson, Elon Musk) and they are usually the one that will make a crowd move to meet them. You can use their name to attract other influencers onboard but they are less likely to respond, promote, or participate. It's not impossible but does require a lot of patience and follow-ups.

b) Trusted Authorities (Medium Visibility/Medium Potential)
This category of speakers usually have a moderate but highly curated subscribers on social media and email list. This is the type of speaker you

want to build relationships with as they are intentionally looking for collaborative strategies to expand their reach (usually have an email list of 5,000-35,000). They are also the most likely to promote to their audience.

c) Rising Stars (Low Visibility/High Potential)
Rising stars are people who have high potential to become an A-type influencer in the near future. It's pretty difficult to gauge this potential, but if they are hustlers and hungry to support your project (and if it makes sense for them to be a speaker), it could be a great addition to the summit.

They also can the high-level employee of a company or influencer you are trying to ultimately reach (e.g Vaynermedia, MindValley, Entrepreneur Organization). Once you've built a genuine relationship with them, it's easier to reach out and ask if they can help you get your dream speaker on the 2.0 version of your summit.

10.3 Where to Find Your Influencers

Personal Network
Existing Customers (if you have that)
Course "Affiliate" Launches
Partner Webinars
Other Virtual Summits
Bloggers In Your Industry
Podcast Hosts
Podcast Guests
Authors
Course Creators
Facebook Groups
LinkedIn Groups
Pinterest
Instagram
YouTube

Bigger Publications
Conferences And Industry Events

10.4 Strategies to Book Your Dream Speakers

a) What to Have Ready Before Reaching Out to Speakers

It's important to have plenty of information/components ready before reaching out to A-type speakers.
- Have several speakers confirmed
- Have landing page ready
- Research their work and upcoming projects

b) Finding Emails

When reaching out to speakers, it's always best to directly contact the speaker themselves. Most emails on a website or 'contact' section are usually managed by an assistant who filters the emails and sends the most important ones to their boss.

To avoid falling into the spam or ignored category, it's critical to land in the speaker's inbox directly to increase your chances of success. Use these tools to do it:

- **Hunter.io (freemium)**

This is one of the most advanced email-finding tools. Hunter.io searches data from a domain name (email formats, email addresses found on the web, verifications and other signals) to find the right contact information in half a second. The free version allows you to do 100 searches per month for free. There are also plenty of alternatives online if you google "alternatives for Hunter.io".

- **Snov.io (freemium)**

This is my go-to software to find emails. Snov.io allows you to find anyone's email based on their LinkedIn profile— as most influencers use their personal email to create their LinkedIn account. It also allows you to see whether your emails have been opened, and sends an automatic follow-up message after couple days to follow-up with the speaker.

c) Power of Follow-Up

My rule is to follow up with a dream speaker up to 7 times via email if they haven't answered you back. You always want to be respectful and keep in mind they are probably dealing with hundreds of similar emails every single day.

But persistence pays off if you are respectful and creative with your process. One of the dream speakers on the Influence Mastery Summit was Peng Joon. They wanted to feature successful national entrepreneurs from their home country and Peng Joon is one of the most followed online marketers in the world (2.1M followers on Facebook) who was born and raised in Kuala Lumpur, Malaysia.

After finding his personal email via Snov.io, our team sent him 3 emails to invite him to be a speaker on our summit— no reply. Not even an opened email. We started to comment on all his latest posts on Facebook, Instagram, and Twitter. Didn't work either.

One of the team members signed up on his webinar just to say hello and continued to engage by adding value to his online community. Peng Joon started to notice but didn't bite yet.

Peng Joon occasionally makes satirical online marketing rap videos and we saw that he just published one on Youtube. That sparked an idea in us. We decided to play on the same field and sent him an invitation rap video to be part of our summit.

Less than 24 hours, he saw our video and said he was impressed by our follow-up game without being too intrusive. He then agreed to be on our summit **for free** when he usually charges over $7,000 for a 1-hour private consultation.

I'm not saying you need to create rap videos to invite all your speakers (but the results and conversion rate would probably be pretty damn high). But a non-response doesn't mean no, it leaves you room to be creative in order to stand out.

Make the other party feel special and wanted without being needy. When reaching out to speakers, you can settle only when you get a hard *No* or *Yes*.

10.5 Steps After Confirming Speakers

a) Pre-Call with Speakers (Optional)

When determining whether a speaker would be a good fit or not, I usually schedule a pre-call with them. On the invitation message, I am careful to not promise them to be a guaranteed speaker but ask if they are interested to *potentially be a speaker* on the summit. It also allows me to connect with my guests and get to know them outside of the business context, even if it's for 10-15 minutes. Keep in mind that big speakers usually won't have the time to do a pre-call but you can still talk with their point of communication to explain how the interview will be conducted.

b) Send Speaker Agreement

It's better to be safe than sorry when it comes to contracts and agreements to avoid bad legal surprises. The most important part of this document is to let your speaker know that you have all the rights on the content— allowing you to sell, promote on social media and repurpose however you would like.

c) Agree on Type of Interview

There are 2 types of interview you can do on a summit: Classic Interview and Presentation/Webinar.

1) Classic Interview

This format is where the host decides on the direction the interview will go. Preparing questions in advance and doing research on their topic will help you to stand out from the crowd. You'd be surprised by the amount of people who only do a quick 15-minute google search on their speaker right before the interview.

When you watch or listen to speakers' past interviews, take note of the topics or questions that have been asked in the past. The best questions are the ones that are unique but still relevant to their field of expertise.

One of my favorite interviewers of all time is Tom Bilyeu, Founder of Quest Nutrition and Impact Theory. One of the things that makes him so great is that he systematically breaks down theoretical wisdom into practical actions steps, which makes it engaging for his audience since they can walk away with knowledge ready to be implemented instantly in their life.

Analyze your favorite interviewer and make a list of charisterics that makes them stand out as a host.

2) Presentation/Webinar Style

This format is the best if you opt for the masterclass type of summit— which is my go-to format. A presentation is often perceived as higher value because there's an intentional focus on teaching the audience on how to achieve something. If you were to host a summit on Facebook Ads, it would be valuable to do a presentation on the *12 Key Components of a High-Converting Ad*, or something like that. You get the idea.

Keep in mind that although the presentation style is preferred, it also requires more preparation from the speaker's side. If you want to aim for an easier Yes, the interview style would be the preferred option.

d) Agree on Summit Topic

Ideally you already have a topic in mind after making your list of speakers. But if you don't, make sure you dedicate enough time to do this well.

I usually give 3 different topic options for my speakers to choose during our pre-call or email exchange. Leave an option for your speaker propose their own topics in case none of yours interest them.

It is also your responsibility to make sure your audience understands why this speaker and interview is a valuable piece of the interview series.

Chapter 11: Setting Up Your Virtual Summit Funnel and Website

In this section you are going to learn:

- How to build the ideal tech to power your summit
- How to craft top-notch pages and forms
- How to write the perfect email sequence
- How to make your pages look the part

The next step is to set up the summit pages and tech system— which can be a little bit intimidating if you are not tech savvy. But don't worry. You will have the tools and steps to build a high-converting funnel that took me years to perfect.

When I built my first virtual summit, I honestly had no idea what I was doing. I didn't know what software to use to send emails, how to host my website, or how to setup the membership site or payment processor. Google was my best friend, and if you are still lost in the process, you can easily find the answers on Youtube or professional blogs that will provide different in-depth explanations.

11.1 Overview of Summit Funnel Pages (Pre-Launch Setup)

(diagram: Summit Funnel Pages overview showing Traffic Source → Registration Push emails → Summit Registration & Playbook PDF Page → Summit One-Time-Offer (OTO) Page → Summit Sales Page / Membership Access All-Access Pass, followed by Pre-Launch Email Sequence + Push for All-Access Pass (Upgrade) and Live Kick-Off Hangout Reminder Emails, leading to Sessions Page, Summit Sales Page, and Kick-Off Live Page)

(courtesy of Navid Moazzez)

This might seem like a lot but it's actually just only 2-3 extra steps compared to any webinar funnel that most people out there build.

You will need to build *3 pages for the pre-launch phase* (landing page, opt-in form, and thank-you page).

You will need to build *4 pages for your summit launch phase* (speaker session, calendar, contact, and sales page)

You will need *2 types of pages for your paying customer* (payment page and membership).

I will guide on how to set up your 9 summit pages and what software to use to set up your funnel.

11.2 Registration Page

It is recommended to build your registration page before reaching out to sponsors and affiliates. It will provide tangible proof that the project is serious and it'll be easier for A-Type speakers to say Yes. It helps even more if you have 4-5 confirmed speakers on the website to give your summit more social proof.

People make a decision about whether they trust you or not in a split second, and design plays a huge role in that. So make sure you prioritize the look of your summit website to make sure it's all cohesive and well-branded.

What is the Role of the Page?
Your registration page is the first page your customers will see when they land on your website. It's the page that gives overall information about your summit and why they need to attend your online conference.
The #1 aim of your summit registration page is to convert your traffic into email subscribers by getting them to register for your summit.

What to Have on the Page
- **Is the logo and summit name clear and explicit?** If your customers have to guess what your summit is about, you already lost most of your traffic.

- **Are the dates and call to action clear and visible** without having to scroll down the page?
- **Who is the target designed for?** Be as precise as possible so that your ideal customer thinks "this is exactly me" when they are on your summit page.
- **What is the outcome for your attendees?** Explain in detail the expected result in their life by attending your event. Basically, tell them "why they should care about your event".
- **Speakers?** Present your experts and include their summit topic under their name so your attendees know ahead of time what to expect.
- **What is a virtual summit?** A lot of people will be attending their first virtual conference. Having a small sections explaining the structure and benefits of attending a virtual summit will help you save time with customer service questions.
- **Who is the host?** Have 1-2 paragraphs about you and why you are hosting the event. You can also share background information and your past accomplishments that led you to this point.

What Tech to Use

I prefer building my summits on Wordpress and also use Thrive Builder to build everything on the website. Everything is pre-built for you and you just need to assemble the pieces like a lego kit. No need to code or reinvent the wheel.

If you are not tech savvy or don't have tech support, you can use funnel builders like Clickfunnel but I personally don't like how restrictive the platform when it comes to design and customer experience.

What Does it Look Like?
- Crypto Virtual Summit.com
- Influence Mastery Summit.com
- Media Mastery Summit.com

11.3 Opt-In Forms

What's the Role of the Page?
Once your summit registration is ready to go, you'll need to add in an opt-in form so people can actually opt in (and be added to your email list) when they click the button to sign up.

What Should I Have on the Page?
- Your summit name and hook
- Form for people to enter their name and email address
- Button to submit details
- Disclaimer with link to your privacy policy (make sure your opt in form is GDPR compliant!)

What Tech Should I Use?
You can use Thrive Builder to build the opt-in form. They offer a vast variety of pre-built forms you can edit and use for your summit.

You also need a CRM to capture your leads. There are several good options like InfusionSoft, XYD or DBNW depending on your budget. I personally like Active Campaign. It's cheap. reliable, and offers a lot of customizable options.

11.4 Thank You and Sales Page

What's the Role of the Page?
The offer page and sales page are your most important revenue generators. The goal is to share the value of the All-Access Pass so attendees upgrade and become paid customers.

The main difference between the offer page and the sales page is the special discount on the offer page that people can only access once after they first register. I usually give a 15-minute discount to people who register for the first time, and explain that the price will never be as low as this offer throughout the entire event.

This creates real urgency for people to upgrade on the offer page, which drives up the conversion rate quite a lot (and allows you to immediately reinvest the pre-sales into your marketing campaign).

What to Have on the Page

- **Confirmation Section**
  After signing up on your landing page, it is important to say they will receive their free ticket in their inbox soon. Some attendees might be confused why there's an offer to buy the All-Access Pass when the ad said the summit is free. Adding this element eliminates any confusion.

- **Why They Should Get the All-Access Pass**
  Interviews are only available for 24 hours and 99.9% of your attendees won't have time to watch everything. Go over the benefits of buying the All-Access Pass to avoid missing out on any valuable content.

- **What's Included in the All-Access Pass**
  Most attendees will buy the pass because of the bonuses. In Chapter 8 we already worked on what type of bonuses you should include in your AAP.

- **Why to Trust You and Your Experts**
  List your confirmed speakers and the topics they'll be covering, plus the results your speakers have been getting, in order to re-establish credibility.

- **30-Day Refund Guarantee**
  Guarantee to take the risk off of them and if they don't like the content, give a 100% refund with no questions asked.

- **Information About the Host**
    Have 1-2 paragraphs about you and why you are hosting the event. You can also share background information and your past accomplishments that led you to this point.

What Tech to Use

For the 15-minute offer, I recommend using Deadline Funnel which tracks the email address AND IP address of each visitor so that people can only access the offer once (even if they try to sign up again with another email address).

It's cloud-based so you don't have to mess around with plugins and really easy to set up. It also automatically adjusts for time zone differences. This has exceptional live support so you can get your automated funnel up and running in no time.

What Does it Look Like?

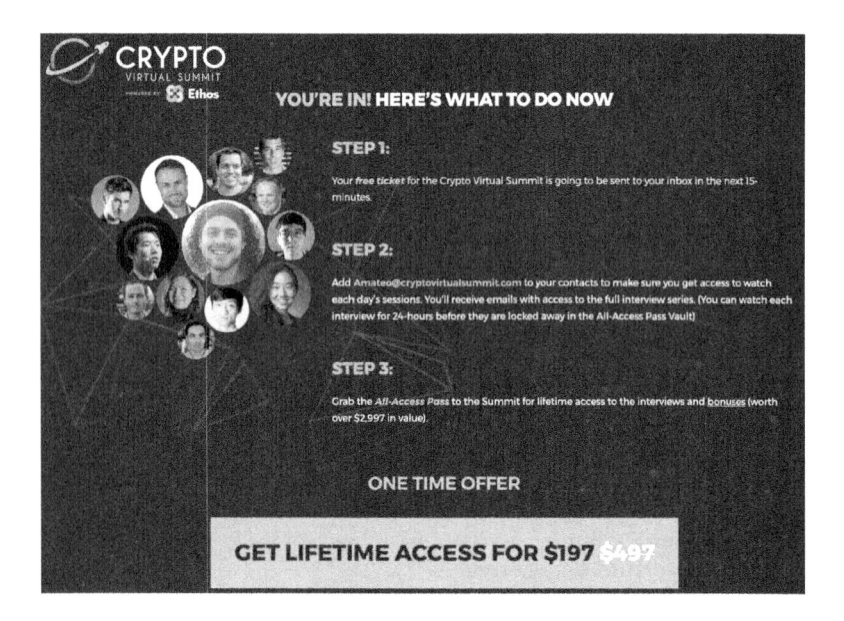

The only difference between the Thank-you page (15-minute offer) and sales page (launch offer) is the pricing. You can duplicate your summit page and set up the sales page in less than 10 minutes.

Typically you want to make the All-Access Pass *25% to 50% more expensive* than the 15-minute offer. If the difference is too small or too big, attendees will either not buy or it will hurt your margins.

Crafting Your Pre-Summit Email Sequence

Once people begin to land on your registration page and sign up for your summit, then what? Well, because you made your 'Thank You' page a sales page, you should see sales begin to roll in.

That will be a great feeling when you start seeing it happen, believe me. However, if this is all you do, *you're still going to miss out on more than 50% of your sales*.

The thing that will actually sell your core offer ("All Access Pass" or otherwise) is the emails sent directly to the new subscribers. So you're going to have to craft a sequence of emails that compel your new subscribers to buy what you're selling.

Here's what I recommend as a *rough* outline of the emails you should send and when:
- Email #1. Thanks for signing up (with a pitch for your "All Access Pass" or core offer in the 'P.S.' area). This should be sent immediately after someone registers for your summit.
- Email #2. What the summit is all about (this is a teaser for the event with a CTA for the "All Access Pass").
- Email #3. Highlight the most important aspect of your offer (this is a direct sales pitch for your "All Access Pass" or core offer).

- Email #4. Tomorrow, this deal goes away! (This is sent the day prior to you raising the price of the "All Access Pass", and/or removing bonuses that are exclusive for early adopters – aka: people who buy now, not later).

11.5 Checkout Page

What's the Role of This Page?
You will need to create a checkout page to accept payments from your customers. Some payment processor allows you to track your affiliates and directly distributes the commission automatically.

What to Have on the Page
- Summit branding and 30-day money back
- Deliverables of the All-Access Pass and what's included in their purchase
- Testimonials for additional social proof and trust
- Simple and easy process for the customer to complete

What Tech to Use
I've used Simplero for a long time, which has a lot of functionality in one (CRM + affiliate + payment processor + membership), but it didn't always perform well on the email side. My new favorite platforms to create checkout forms is ThriveCart or Kartra. It takes me 15 minutes to create my checkout pages and connect it to my Paypal or Stripe account.

Pro Tip: Reach out to your payment processor and bank ahead of time to let them know you are expecting to receive a large amount of money into your account. Some payment processors block your account to check for potential fraudulent transaction (although it doesn't happen often). It's better to be safe than sorry, as I've witnessed many launches where the host couldn't receive money from potential customers.

What Does it Look Like?

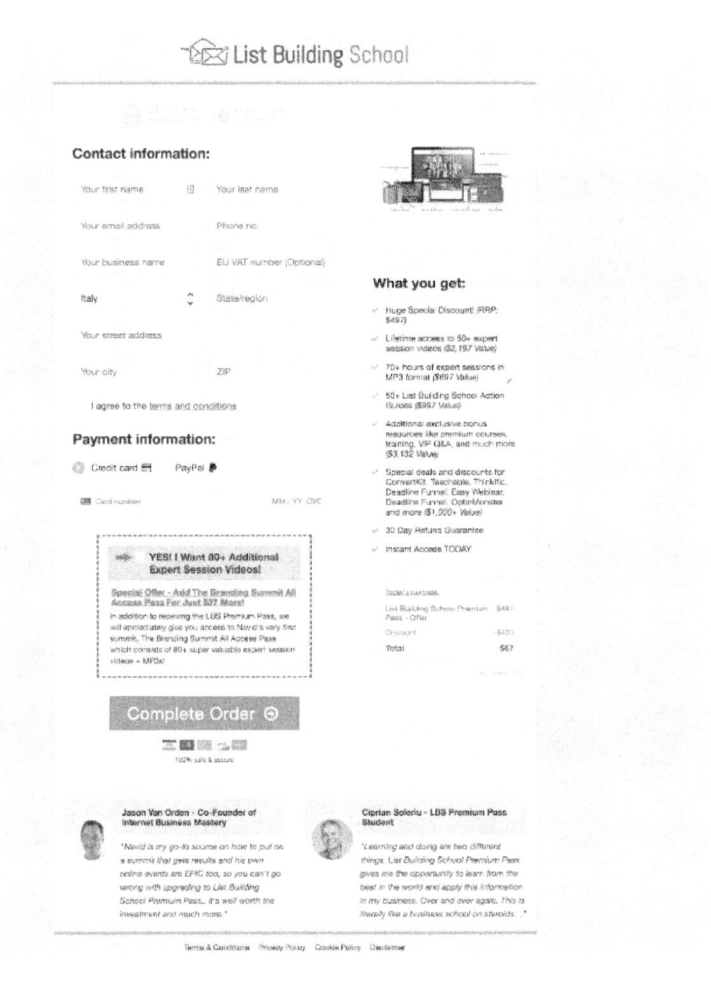

11.6 Inner Pages (When Summit Starts)

What's the Role of the Page?
Now that all your pre-summit pages have been created, there are only a few pages left that needs to be set up for your summit to be fully operational.

You only need 3 pages for that step:

a) **Calendar:** This page is where you can hold the currently available interviews for viewing. You'll list each of the day's speakers, their topics, and links to access each interview.

OUR PRESENTATIONS

These presentations will only be available for a limited time!

Upgrade Now – ONLY $197

Phase 3 – Monetizing
Day 11, Thursday, July 23

03	06	24	20
day	hour	minute	second

These interviews are available until July 26 at 8:59pm EST (72 hours from when last interview of the day goes live)

Jaime Tardy
Building My Business & Group Coaching Program Through My First Book (The Eventual Millionaire Book Case Study)
View Session

Russell Brunson
Using a book to sell more software & information products. 25,000 Books, a Ferrari, and $500,000+ in Backend Revenue. Here's How I Did It...
View Session

Brian Tracy
"Before Book" vs. "After Book" (B.B. vs A.B.): Doubling Your Income By Writing Your First Book
View Session

Chandler Bolt
Summit Recap: How to Write, Market & Publish Your First Book In 90 Days or Less (LIVE Closing Keynote, 9PM EST)
View Session

b) Speaker Page

This page is where you will be hosting the interviews. You can create a template and duplicate each page for every speaker you have on your summit. This is a basic page we used on the Crypto Virtual Summit:

It's recommended to host the interview videos on Vimeo and make it semi-private so that only the people who registered for the summit can access the video (without being able to download them). You can also manually remove the videos from the internet once the day is finished if you prefer.

You can also add:

- A comments section for attendees to share their thoughts
- CTA to buy the All-Access Pass
- The speakers' social media links and resources mentioned from the interview

c) **Support Page**

This will be a standard contact page for your support team to be used by any attendees who have questions.

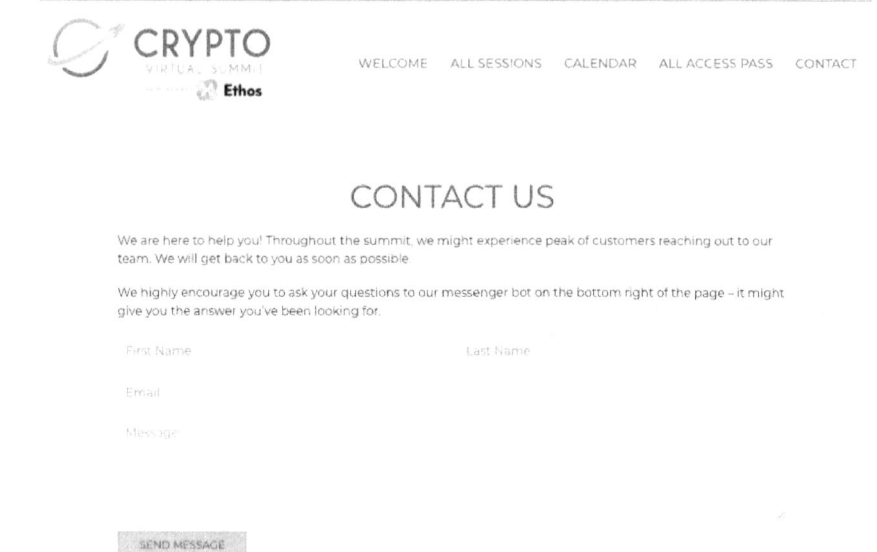

I generally also add a 'Frequently Asked Questions' section under the 'Contact Us' section because many of your customers will have the same questions. You can save up to 90% of your time replying to emails by creating a FAQ page.

11.7 Membership Site

Here you will host all lifetime access videos. These pages need to be password protected so only those attendees who purchase your premium pass can view them.
There are several options for you to host the videos:
- Teachable
- Kartra
- Any Wordpress membership plugin (MemberPress or S2Member)

If you aren't tech savvy, I recommend using a platform that has 90% of the membership site pre-built for you. Wordpress plugin is generally free or a 1-time payment, but the risk is not always having a point of contact if your integration stops working.

Your membership site should include the following concepts:
- Organize into sections. Our team organized the crypto summit into 3 sections (foundations, investing, future of blockchain technologies). The membership site and interviews were organized into these sections as well.

- The visual look can be similar to the pages you designed on your summit page. The only difference is that these pages will stay on the membership site for life, while the speaker pages on the summit will be removed after 24-72 hours (whatever time you have decided to make the videos available).

CRAFTING YOUR PRE-SUMMIT EMAIL SEQUENCE

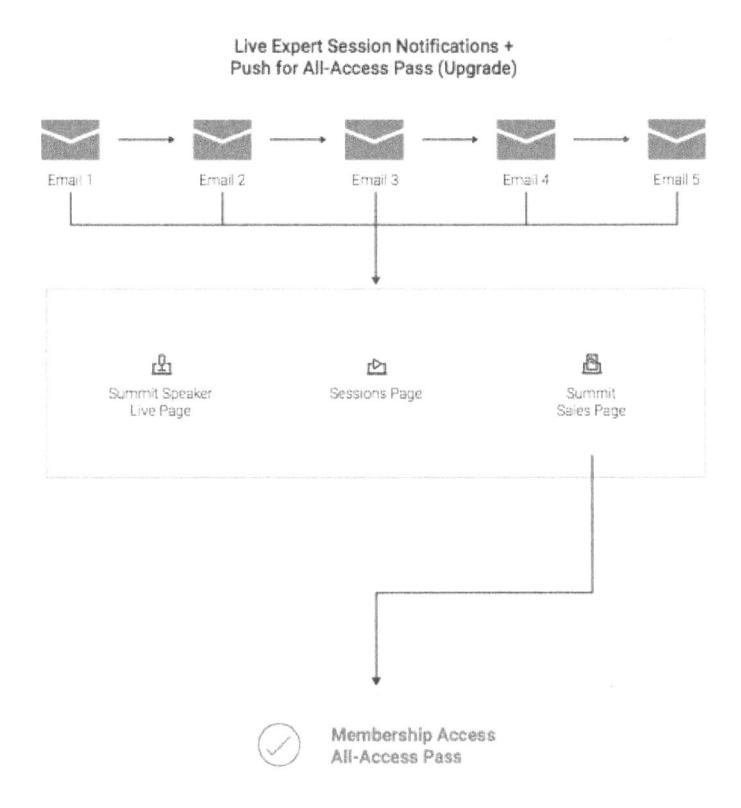

[Diagram: Email 1 → Email 2 → Email 3 → Email 4 → Email 5 — Live Expert Session Notifications + Push for All-Access Pass (Upgrade). Emails link to Summit Speaker Live Page, Sessions Page, and Summit Sales Page. Summit Sales Page leads to Membership Access / All-Access Pass.]

11.8 Quality Control Everything

Schedule an *entire week* at the end of this phase (the month before your summit launches) to go over every single asset you've created and double check it.
Look over all of the following:
- Make sure all web pages, copy, emails, communication schedule, videos, sign-up/registration process, all mobile pages, payment

confirmation system and pages, and all processes are processing correctly
- Make sure all content is ready on inner pages (Get a second pair of eyes to help with this!)
- Make sure your email service provider is integrated with your sign-up form
- Test all pages, sign-ups, payments, and email automations
- Now test all of this again on a mobile device
- Now test all of this again with different browsers

Chapter 12: Sponsors

In this section you are going to learn:

- How to gain sponsors without any connections by making the perfect offer
- How to reverse-engineer the top-performing sponsorship packages
- How to do outreach that *won't be ignored*
- How to close the loop to guarantee outcome

You can download the sponsorship deck we used to raise $75,000 in sponsorship on leadnextgen.com/book-bonus

---

Sponsorship is one of the most underutilized strategies to finance your virtual summit launch. **All your tech expenses can be covered** if you get just 1 or 2 sponsors. Most people don't think about getting sponsors because they treat virtual summits as an advanced version of a webinar. But the correct perspective is treating your event as the digital version of those ultra-popular live events.

And if you go to big events, you must have seen the long list of partners and sponsors who pay well over $10K just to have a small booth— because they know the returns can be exponentially higher.

This is how all the online events I've helped launch were **100% self-funded through sponsorship**. We spent $0 from our own pocket (even for websites) and all the funds went directly into our marketing budget.

You don't need to be well-connected or have an established list to get sponsors.

I've started with:

- No speakers
- No email list or social media presence
- No pre-established relationships
- No offers
- No partners

And it didn't stop me from raising $5,000 on my first summit. $23,000 on my second. Over $75,000 on my third. And that's *without even counting the sales we had during and after the event.*

I've taught many summit hosts how to replicate the system I'm about to share with you— and how you can launch a profitable summit before you even start.

And it starts with 4 Key Elements:
1. The offer (What could we offer in return for sponsorship money? i.e. what could we sell?)
2. The prospects (Who might take you up that offer?)
3. The outreach (How can I get in touch with everyone in a short period of time?)
4. The deal (Convincing people to sponsor us with cold hard cash)

12.1 The Offer

Everything in business is a transaction. It's an exchange. And one thing that drives me crazy with nonprofits and fundraising is what I call the "beggar mentality".

You're bound to have seen it. It's where people say, "I want to raise money, please give me some". It's just fancy begging.

It doesn't matter how amazing your product, service, idea, or business is. You can repel people with this approach. You're not offering value— or at least, you're not communicating that value well to others.

It's also a far more powerful position to come from when you have something of value. When it's limited or scarce, you can use "prizing" to your benefit. It's going to be much easier to generate interest and get sponsors and money if you have an attractive offer.

In every successful partnership and every business, even massive brands like Nike have something that they need. It's your job to find an intersection between what others need and what you have.

For larger brands, a successful partnership might mean having money in the bank to pay for exposure via advertising. Others will need to leverage assets like the strength of their branding or audience. Or it could be something as simple as your expertise, or even having an office space people want to use. The idea is to look at what assets you have that would offer value to others, and use it to help you get what you need.

For the Crypto Virtual Summit, we had a platform gathering potentially over 10,000 crypto enthusiasts who wanted to learn directly from top blockchain companies— perfect for smaller companies that want to be featured next to industry giants.

For the Airbnb Mastery Summit, we attracted a community of real estate and short-term rentals businessman who wanted to learn how to optimize their businesses— perfect for real estate Saas or products designed to help manage properties better.

Next, we made it compelling by pricing it very aggressively so that it was extremely competitive and offered excellent value.

We knew that if someone wanted to advertise to our ideal demographic, we could put them in front of our audience and as a bonus contribute a bit of an added halo effect from our brand.

Make a list of all the advantages and offer your virtual summit would give to their company if they invested in your event. You can also download the sponsorship package from the Airbnb Mastery Summit here.

How to Get Sponsored and Make This Work for You

If you want to know how to get sponsored, simply look at what you have that you can offer.

Things such as: speaker advertising, social mentions, an email broadcast to your subscribers, product reviews, creating content, products, expertise, member specials, workshops, events... what can you offer that has value to them?

Next, ensure that your offer is extremely compelling as well as competitively priced. This makes it far easier for you to pitch and sell— even if you are not very good at sales. Add in extras and be ready to negotiate.

Exercise: Research the top live events in your industry, get ahold of their sponsorship packages, and analyze what they have to offer at what price point— then reverse engineer what already works on your summit.

It's also easier to pitch to sponsors who have already invested in the past. Reach out to a couple and asked them about their experience from 1 to 10 at *X* event. Even if they say 10, ask what would have made it even better.

If they are wondering why they would share that information, you can say you are thinking about becoming a sponsor next year and wanted to get feedback from previous years' sponsors.

Once you have found what most of the companies are looking for, you can offer the same thing but at a no-brainer price point.

You can also trade exposure for work and sponsorship for appearance on your summit. For my first summit, I traded a speaker and sponsorship spot in exchange for designing the entire summit build for me.

Vision Tech Team (now Influex) wanted to train their new employees on a project that was low risk (since it was pro-bono). But they were also focused on establishing their brand as the go-to web design agency that serves online marketing influencers.

The summit helped them get in front of their ideal customers —my speakers— and 4 of them ended up hiring Influex to build their website. One of their premium services now costs as high as $60,000.

Not all of them chose the premium service but the math is pretty simple. They got new clients and I got a free website. Win-win situation.

12.2 The Prospects

As we craft our offer, we have a fairly good idea of who might take it up. Some of our speakers on the Airbnb Summit were also ideal sponsors.

Next on the Airbnb Summit, I worked with our VA to look at the top podcasts in our space, and found out which ones had advertising so we could look for highly qualified prospects to approach.

She created a list of who was already paying for advertising, and which podcasts they were advertising on. This is a great place to start. We then created a list of contacts and emails for those companies. That was only 10-20 prospects, so we needed a bigger list— and went to do the same work for live conferences in our industry.

The question was: who would want to get in front of our audience and be a good match for our brand? We quickly decided that SaaS companies and tools that were funded would:

a) Be interested in growth

b) Have advertising budgets

This was something I learned from working in the blockchain space. A lot of companies have a great product and plenty of money dedicated to advertising, but don't know how to spend their money in order to actually get in front of their ideal customers.

Some blockchain companies invest their time and money into events but the biggest pain point was not having any trackable data from the huge investment they made. At a live event the number of seats and attendees is limited, but sponsors pay the same amount whether the event has 200 or 500 attendees (and are heavily dependent on the organizers to have quality).

This is where we knew our Crypto Virtual Summit could add tremendous value to most blockchain companies.

So we reached out to over 200 CEOs and Founders who spoke at and sponsored live events. **We presented a far better ROI by having virtually**

no limits on the number of participants at our event (since it's online), but also offered them trackable data on the event performances.

They loved the idea of the conference being remote, especially since a lot of crypto enthusiasts don't have the time to sacrifice a weekend to physically attend a conference. And more people nowadays in other industries feel the same, too.

Here's an example of the spreadsheet we used:

Nothing fancy, just a spreadsheet. But pay attention, because things are about to get interesting. Make sure you have the fields "Company Name," "First Name," "Last Name," and "Email" if you want to follow my methodology and marketing from the "How to Get Speakers" section to find their emails.

If you get very clear on your target customer/sponsor, it should be pretty easy to put together a list of people who are already paying for sponsorships, as well as companies that might be interested.

12.3 The Outreach

Time to get our hands a little dirty.

No one likes cold calls. No one likes cold emails either... unless that email is highly targeted, compelling, and has something that they want. But let's be real. Getting attention in someone's inbox still isn't easy.

As you read this, you may be tempted to think: "Sure, but you've done many summits so it's easy for you. I don't have a list."

Well, to some random person working at a SaaS company who hasn't heard of me, let's just politely say that they don't care. They have other things to do.

Therein lies the biggest, two-headed challenge. First, we need to contact 200 or so people. It needs to be a decent number because, like any sales or partnership funnel, out of that 200 maybe 40% open the email, 20% reply, and then 5-10% actually end up becoming a potential partner.

The heart of outreach at scale is that it still needs to be personal, otherwise it will be ignored. People are always on the lookout for bulk messages, and they burn them on sight. But a Gmail, with their name, company, and email all referenced? Well that's a little more personal.

That buys you a few extra seconds of their attention and will at least increase your chances that they'll open it.

Something like this:

> **Hello **If Name***,**
>
> I am reaching out to offer a personal invitation to be a speaker on our upcoming online seminar for Cryptocurrency and Blockchain - the Crypto Virtual Summit.
>
> It would be an honor to have you and (insert company*) be represented on the Summit. This is the premiere online seminar and conference for the crypto and blockchain industry.
>
> We only have a few spots left, and I wanted to see if you are interested to speak - only requires 1-hour of your time. We expect and audience of over 10,000 people - who we can share (insert company*) mission and message too.
>
> We would love to help you reach more people - and spread awareness of your company.
>
> **Here are just a few of the Speakers we have confirmed:**
> - Ben Yu, Founder of Stream
> - Shingo Lavine, Founder of Bitquence
> - Eyal Herzog CEO of Bancor
> - Ameer Rosic, Block Geeks
> - Mance Hamon, Co-Founder of Hashgraph + Swirlds
> - Amy Wan, Bootstrap Legal
> - Jane Lippencott of Zen Cash
> - Lindsay Maule, Precursor VC
> - Richard Ma of Quantstamp
> - Thomas Shouten of Lisk
>
> If you are interested - let's schedule quick chat to discuss having you join the Summit. I will share with you how it all works, it's very easy and efficient - and explore if your company would be a good fit for our audience
>
> **Next Step:** Here is the link to his calendar to set up an info chat:
> https://calendly.com/amateora/crypto-virtual-summit-connection-call/
>
> Thank you so for your time!
> ~ Amateo
>
> Crypto Virtual Summit

The body of the email is **crucial**. It needs to be short, snappy, and not ask for too much. It's important to pique curiosity, but if you tell them the whole deal, they will make a lizard-brain decision.

"Uh-oh. This guy wants money. Too hard. Not interested". When in reality, we have an extremely competitive and well-priced deal, we know we have what they want, and it's a better offer than what they're used to.

So that's not the response we want. My goal is simply to advance the conversation. Not to land the deal.

So the ask was just to get on a Skype call to find out if we had an offer that would suit them, talk them through their needs, and see if we could help. I also use scarcity tactics by limiting the number of sponsors we would take on (different email version for that).

That should be your goal of the outreach. Get an open. Get a response. Move the deal forward one step.

12.4 The Deal

When asking for $5,000+ from strangers, you're going to need to put in some face time. After following up, the next step is to have a video call with them.

This can get messy. They were busy. I was busy. Time zones didn't work, and remember I had about 200 people in the starting pipeline. Working in Asia and straining to do midnight calls to Europe or the US seriously limited me.

Again, this is where I had technology do the heavy lifting for me.

I use an awesome scheduler called Calendly. It allows me to easily let people book in a time with me (when I was free), add it to my calendar, send reminders, and even force them to pre-qualify by filling out a form. Just awesome. Highly recommended.

The best approach was to see it as a "partnership" and not a sales call.
- The call structure was basically intro and pleasantries first
    - What do you guys do?
    - What would help you (what do you need)?
- Here's what we have (with good homework, this should match exactly what they need)

- The close (are you interested?)

Post call:
- Next steps (summarize the call in the email)
- Reach an agreement, send the contract, and ask them to wire the sponsorship money

There was no sneaky sales script. Being authentic works well, but you still need to ensure that they understand the value of what you have and how it can truly help them.

So, there you have it, simple!

Not necessarily easy. But it can totally be done.

Chapter 13: How to Run Your Summit

In this section you are going to learn:

- How get subscribers and sales *straight out of the gate*
- How to tap into using affiliates to your advantage
- How to run ads that *work*
- How to leverage pre-existing communities in your favor

At this point, you've got your topic selected, your speakers recruited, and your pages set up. Now it's time to kick things off and actually run the summit.

A summit can be broken down into three phases:
Phase 1: Pre-summit
Phase 2: Live Event
Phase 3: Post-summit

Phase 1: PRE-SUMMIT (Promotion)

During the pre-summit phase, you want two things to happen:
- Get new subscribers
- Get sales of your "All Access Pass" (or core offer)

Here's the nice part about a virtual summit: if you can accomplish #1 above, #2 will follow as a result. So your time and energy should be spent on doing whatever it takes to get new subscribers. Since you already have your landing page ready, that means you just need one thing: traffic. And you can drive traffic in plenty of different ways.

Your Personal Network

The idea is to let anyone who is already familiar with your brand know about your summit so that they can help you to start getting momentum and initial traction for your event.

One of the most powerful things you can do to get some momentum is to reach out to your personal network to get your first 100-200 summit opt-ins for free.

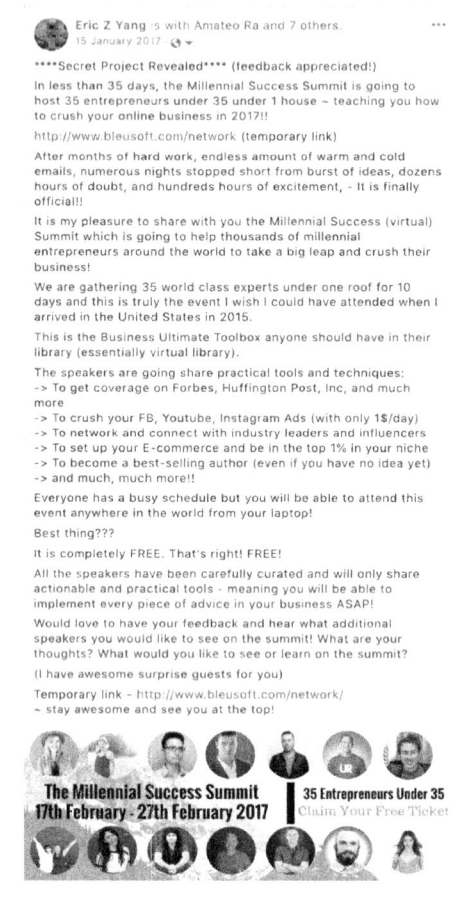

This post added 78 new attendees in less than 3 hours, and I updated on Facebook every 3 days to remind people what I was working on.

It was very intimidating for me to share what I was doing, at least at the very beginning. But that feeling of getting your first few signups and sales for your summit is absolutely incredible.

Feel free to use these platforms to your advantage for sharing:
- Facebook (personal page, business page, groups)
- Instagram
- Reddit
- Twitter
- LinkedIn

Affiliates

Just because someone said they would share doesn't mean they WILL share. And it's not because they're a bad person, because they hate you all of a sudden, or because they decided that now, when the campaign is underway, that they don't want to be associated with you...

No, the reason your partners won't promote is because:

- They're busy
- You're making things difficult

That's it.

That's why it is critical to be SUPER CLEAR with your affiliates so they know when and how to promote. It's your job as the summit host to make it ridiculously easy for affiliates to share your summit to their community.

How Much Commission?

50-50 revenue share is industry standard for summit speakers and partners (plus 20-50% commission for upsales).

How Long are Their Link Clicks Valid?

They should be credited for the sale even if someone purchases later (e.g. 60-365 day cookie period, or even lifetime).

What Can They Share?
Affiliates can share your free registration. They should get an affiliate link for each page they can promote.

What Should I Have on my Affiliate Page?
- Introduction to your summit (purpose, speakers etc.)
- Reasons to participate as an affiliate
- Launch schedule (important dates etc.)
- Commission and payment details
- Promotion and tools pack
- Affiliate contest details and tips
- Rules for affiliates
- About you/the summit host
- How to sign up as an affiliate

> **Tip #1: Treat each affiliate as if they are the laziest person on the planet with the attention span of a goldfish.**

Let's start with the obvious: no, they're not lazy, and yes, they can focus for more than 3 minutes.

The reason you should still pretend is because it'll force you to make things as easy, simple, and frictionless as possible for affiliates to promote your summit.

For example: the laziest person on the planet doesn't want to have to create a new account on some random platform, spend 30 minutes writing promotional email with no guideline, and lose their minds over what the correct link is to use— just to send one email.

No, the laziest person on the planet would rather have it all done for them so they have to do nothing.

Make it so simple that even an 8-year old could do it by giving them exactly what they need, when they need it, so they only have to copy, paste, and send.

If you want them to send an email, give them the EXACT email they need to send with their affiliate links already integrated, and make sure it's within the body of the email you send their way (assuming you're using email to communicate, which is preferable for this).

Bottom line: don't make your speakers and affiliates jump through hoops. Give them everything they need, ready to go, neatly and on time (with lots of reminders for good measure).

> **Tip #2: The power is in the follow-up (and follow-up. And following up again).**

Persistence pays off.
When it comes to getting speakers to promote and share your summit, the same rules apply.

Just because someone agreed to share your summit 6 months ago doesn't mean you're good to go now. You need to follow up, probably at least once a month in the lead-up to the summit, and every week in the month before a summit. Then you need to follow up every few days during the summit (during the pre-summit and live-event phases at least).

> **Tip #3: Create an amazing affiliate customer experience.**

Just like it's important to provide great customer service to get buyers talking about your company, it's important to provide great affiliate service to get your network talking about your program.

The more reasons they have to boast how great the partnership is, the more potential affiliates will come your way.

Communication is key to making them feel involved and respected, as well as working with them on content projects and initiatives. In short, keep in mind the **3 C's of good affiliate relationships: Communication. Collaboration. Commission**.

While having competitive commission rates is a no-brainer to attracting and retaining good affiliates, another aspect of paying out percentages is to do it quickly. Nothing, and we mean nothing, kills the buzz around your network faster than late checks.

Under-promise, over-deliver. It's good practice to put in your terms and conditions that commissions are paid out at, say, 30 days; but actually deliver the checks in 25. It does wonders for the morale of your network and will get them buzzing about how great your program is to their friends.

And even if you stick to the net 30, just never be late. It's a simple and effective way to ingratiate affiliates new and old to your program.

> **Tip #4: Leverage live events and online communities.**

Attending industry meet and greets, hosting your own event, and hitting local business conferences are great ways to bring in new affiliates. Just make sure you go prepared with the right materials to bring them in. If you have a booth, make affiliate reach a priority by having "become an affiliate" signage. If not, business cards and pamphlets and branded merch can all be used to spread awareness about your program. Have your 2-minute elevator pitch ready:

> *"Hey, our affiliate program is looking for new partners. We pay the highest commissions in our industry with bonuses for X sales, and access to exclusive products."*

If you're going to be at these events anyway, you might as well take advantage of all the interested individuals swarming around.

Your followers on Facebook are worth their virtual weight in gold. More than Twitter or Instagram, those who take the time to join your business group or like your page are not only more engaged than anywhere else, you have a great platform to engage with them about your affiliate program.

Regularly post about your affiliate program, including success stories (as in your newsletter). It's a low-effort way to create buzz among the people who have already raised their hand in favor of your business.

Also, it's an easy way for your best affiliates to share their own stories directly with your audience to increase trust in your brand and in the program itself. This is especially good for smaller businesses who might not be able to get out to live events very often. Spending 30 minutes a day communicating with fans on Facebook can lead to a solid pipeline of potential affiliate partners.

Tip #5: Contest

Pete Vargas launched a $3,000,000 virtual summit to teach entrepreneurs how to get booked and paid to speak on stages.

One of his most successful marketing strategies was having a big affiliate network promoting his content. These huge affiliate networks knew ahead of time what the conversion rates of his programs were, and could easily calculate the ROI by promoting to their email list.

To incentivize affiliates to promote multiple times, he created a contest rewarding affiliates for 2 of his most desired outcomes: Leads and Sales

> We Will Be Offering
> **TWO UN-FREAKIN-BELIEVABLE AFFILIATE CONTESTS**
> That You Can Participate In For The
> **"STAGE TO SCALE METHOD" LAUNCH**
>
> Click On The Contest Tabs Below For Complete Details.
>
> **OPT-IN CONTEST:**
> $115,600 In Cash And Prizes
>
> **SALES CONTEST:**
> $505,500 In Cash And Prizes

His top affiliate would get $200,000 worth of prizes ($50,000 cash + $150,000 in masterminds and events).

Even if you don't have $50,000 in cash to give away, you can still create attractive offers such as:
- A VIP Dinner with you and your speakers
- Offering your services for free (mastermind or retreat)
- Goodies from your speakers and sponsors
- Free sponsorsorship feature on summit 2.0
- Consulting and strategy session with you

Get creative and inspire yourself from your competitors' affiliate programs to create your own.

Facebook Ads

Understanding how to leverage Facebook Ads is becoming a staple part of almost every social media strategy. It is essential to have control of your success by not relying on someone else's email list or action to drive traffic to your summit.

Paid advertising on Facebook is one of the most immediate ways to impact the reach your audience online. Although I recommend hiring a Facebook Ads expert to run your marketing campaign, it is important to learn the fundamentals to understand the metrics.

Step 1: Set Some Goals for Your Facebook Ads
Before you jump in and create any adverts, it's important to first think about why you're advertising and what you're aiming to achieve. By setting yourself a few goals ahead of going live with ads, you also have something to measure your success against.

This will also help you when it comes to choosing the correct objective for your Facebook Ads campaign in Step 3 below.

Some more example goals could be:
- Increase traffic to my website from Facebook
- Increase attendance at my event
- Generate new leads
- Increase the reach of our content on Facebook
- Boost engagement for our Facebook Page

Step 2: Design Facebook Ads
Designing coherent ads is critical to obtaining optimal conversion rates. If you hired a web designer, I would recommend asking them to design Facebook ads as well. They should be:
- Eye catching (e.g. color, shapes, layout)
- To the point/clear what it is about

- Different from other ads
- Headshots of influencers
- Congruent with landing page

Here are some examples of ads our Facebook ads manager, Jack Haldrup, used on our summit:

ERIC MOELLER
Host | Airbnb Mastery Summit

THAN MERRILL
CEO | Fortune Builders

FREE TICKET BELOW   AIRBNB MASTERY SUMMIT   **ONLINE EVENT AUG. 11-13**

Text:

> Look, have you ever wondered: "Do people really make money with Airbnb?"... Join me as I host Than Merrill and 20 other experts in the field to discover how people are using Airbnb to make money, right now.. Best of all, your ticket is completely FREE!

FB Ads targeted to Than Merrill:
Amount Spent: $1,077
CPL: $1.47
Total Leads: 731

FB Ads targeted to Interest:
Interests: HomeAway, Expedia, Inc., Expedia (website), Vacation rental, Airbnb, VRBO®- Vacation Rentals By Owner®, Lonely Planet, TripAdvisor, Hotels.com, Trivago or Booking.com

Amount Spent: **$10,948.32**
CPL: $2.76
Total Lead: 3,967
Reach: 255,330

Last Day to Sign Up!
Join our Free Virtual Summit to learn ... Sign Up
AirbnbMasterySummit.com

Text:

Look, have you ever wondered: "Do people really make money with Airbnb?"

Well, me too! So, I set out to interview 20+ experts to find out exactly how much people are making with Airbnb and how real estate investors are adopting the new niche!

My name is Eric Moeller. I'm a successful real estate investor OBSESSED with Airbnb! Ever since my first Airbnb experience in Iceland I realized the tremendous income potential in running a professional Airbnb property!

Fast forward a few years to today and I now run multiple Airbnb's in Southern California and eager to grow into more and more units!

During this FREE online-event I sit down and interview the top experts in short-term rentals, Airbnb and real estate investing to learn how they are making money on Airbnb right now...

Short-term rental experts like Scott Sharford, Sean Conway, Alex Nigg, and Heather Bayer share their knowledge and experience on how to go from one to multiple Airbnb listings and how to successfully and professionally run a STR business.

Top real estate experts like Than Merrill, Kent Clotheir, David Lindahl, J Massey, share their tips and tricks on growing successful investment companies and how investors are adapting Airbnb as a new investment model in their portfolios.

Gain access to these experts for FREE Aug.11-13th and hear what they say about Airbnb and the home-share movement by signing up below!

Looking forward to seeing you on the summit!

P.S.— LIKE and SHARE this post for a chance to win a FREE (VIP TICKET) ALL-ACCESS PASS that comes with over $2,000 in bonuses!

Step 3: Choose Your Ad Placements

Advert placement defines where your ad is shown and with Facebook Ads, you're able to choose which locations your advert will appear in. Adverts may appear in Facebook's mobile News Feed, desktop News Feed and right column. You may also create ads to appear on Instagram.

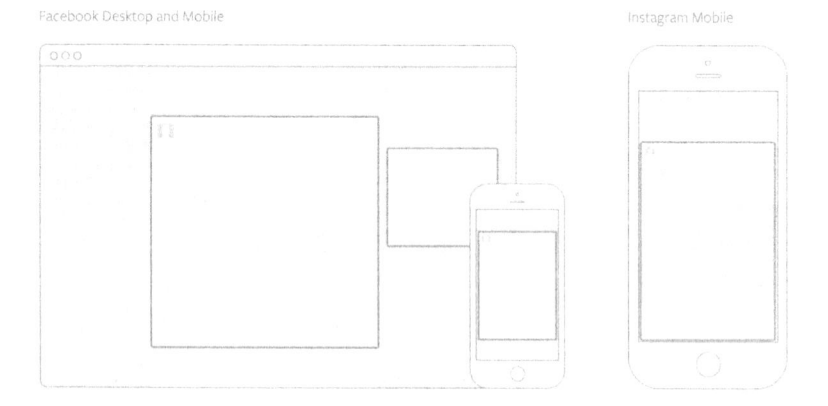

Facebook Desktop and Mobile   Instagram Mobile

Facebook recommend using the default placements for the objective you chose, which enables Facebook to optimize placements for you in order to get the best possible results at the cheapest overall average cost.

However, if you want to select your own placements, Facebook recommend the following choices, broken out by campaign objective:

- **Increase Brand Awareness** campaigns (including Reach and Frequency buying): Facebook and Instagram
- **Boost Your Posts** (including Reach and Frequency buying): Facebook and Instagram
- **Get Video Views** (including Reach and Frequency buying): Facebook and Instagram
- **Get Installs of Your App:** Facebook and Instagram
- **Increase Engagement in Your App:** Facebook
- **Promote a Product Catalog:** Facebook
- **Increase Conversions on Your Website:** Facebook
- **Send People to Your Website:** Facebook

Chapter 14: Post-Summit

In this section you are going to learn:

- How to continue generating sales after the event
- How to curate an ongoing community
- How to produce quality content with minimum time input
- How to make your summit Evergreen and poised for relaunch

Too many people make the mistake of thinking a virtual summit is the event, campaign, or promotion. It's not (or at least it shouldn't be). **What comes immediately *after* your summit is what really matters.** Selling hundreds of all-access passes is great, but your attendees are craving more from you.

This is your chance to turn virtual summit visitors into loyal customers, clients, and fans. And you can do this a number of ways:

#1 OFFER AN UPSELL

- You can offer high-ticket coaching (e.g a 12-week program)
- Do you have a digital products like e-course? Offer that to your audience
- Running a membership site or SaaS company? Give people a 'no-brainer' reason to sign up for a year of access
- Thinking about hosting an event? Pre-sell your conference before putting a deposit down

You want to strike while the iron is hot. Most of your leads spent over 3 days attending your online conference— they are burning hot and ready to buy more from you. Many have been paying attention to what you're doing and are interested in working with you in a deeper capacity.

If you flake on making an offer for your flagship course, product, or service after your summit comes to an end, you just wasted a ton of time, money, and energy. Sure, you could have run a profitable summit, maybe even reached 6 or 7 figures....

But you missed out on the MAJOR opportunity to serve your community. With the right post-summit sequence, you should be able to multiply your profits by 5 to 10x in the months following a campaign.

#2 OFFER A DOWNSELL

Like the upsell described above, a downsell is another opportunity to generate additional revenue, but this time from those who did not purchase your initial offer.

There's typically a 10–20% increase in revenue by offering a downsell to those who don't purchase my initial offer.

Let's say your initial offer is an "All Access Pass" (with whatever bonuses you've included to spice things up).

Those who make a purchase get your upsell offer...
But what about those who don't purchase?

In a given campaign, that's likely to be upwards of 90% of your email list (true story).

So in any given launch, the vast majority of people will never see your offer... and the vast majority of those who DO see your offer still won't buy. That's not good, right?

Well, here's what you can do to nudge people from the category of 'just looking around' to a happy customer.

→ DOWNSELL OPTION 1: OFFER A PAYMENT PLAN FOR YOUR CORE OFFER

For instance, if you're selling your "All Access Pass" for $197 during the summit, you could present a 'flash payment plan offer" at the end of your summit where someone can get access for only $27/month for 8 months (or $47 for 4 months; or $77 for 3 months...you get the idea).

My clients have seen anywhere from a 5% to a 15% bump in overall sales and revenue when we implement this strategy.

The best part is that it's simple and you can execute with minimal effort. All you have to do is create a special checkout cart or coupon code for the payment plan offer, and write one or two emails around this limited-time payment plan offer, then click send. Boom– big boost in revenue (and profit) with very little work on your part.

→ DOWNSELL OPTION 2. OFFER A RELEVANT BUT LESS EXPENSIVE PRODUCT

After you've made multiple offers, appealed to scarcity and urgency, and stacked your bonuses – there are still readers/viewers/subscribers who have NOT purchased your "All Access Pass" (for shame).

Perhaps this person is not interested in all the great interviews you've conducted, but he'd still like to get started working on his small project... well, why not offer him a 'starters guide' eBook on the subject? Something you could sell for under $19 or $29 (one time only, flash discount offer)? Something like this is sure to sell (to at least a portion of your audience).

Now, this offer doesn't have to be an eBook. The point here is it should be less expensive to purchase than the initial or core offer you originally made. In addition, the best downsell offer is something that would help out the beginner just getting started (especially because that's the person who is most likely interested, but doesn't have the money to invest in your original offer– or at least they haven't been convinced to spend it yet).

Curating Community (FB + Email Sequence)

Most summits reach a peak of engagements but fall flat after some time. It's essential to keep the communication alive with your new community—whether it's via social media or email.

You need to actively present and continue to provide value over time, and people will notice and truly appreciate your effort.

Sending an email every 7 days with the biggest lessons you learned that week or sharing key takeaways from the summit are 2 of many possibilities. It is important to have a "home" where your community can gather in between your programs or summit launch.

Survey Audience

A post summit survey can be extremely useful to guide the next decisions in your business. For the Crypto Virtual Summit, we surveyed our audience via Google Form to learn areas of improvement for our next summit and validate other products or service ideas we could offer.

Questions You Can Inspire Yourself with:
1. Why did you buy the All-Access Pass?
2. If you didn't buy the All-Access Pass, what was the reason?
    a. Too expensive
    b. Didn't need it right now

      c. Recordings and/or bonuses weren't interesting enough
      d. The offer wasn't clear
      e. Other
3. Which topics would you like to see covered on our next summit?
4. What do you think we could improve about the summit?
5. Would you recommend this event to a friend?

Example of the email we sent to our audience:

CRYPTO VIRTUAL SUMMIT
POWERED BY
Ethos

Hey hey!

I need your help real quick, but first I need to ask you a question.

Do you hate me? :-)

I'm asking because the last week I gave you a chance to get the Crypto All-Access Pass but for some reason you passed.

Did I not do a good job of explaining something?

Did I not do a good job of touching on a specific hot point that matters to you?

Maybe it was because of me. . .

Something I said, something I didn't say.

In other words, do you hate me?

If you could just do me a favor and click on the link below to let me know. . .

What was the biggest reason you decided not to try the All-Access Pass?

It would really mean the world to me! The entire Crypto Virtual Summit could have be watched for free and we would love to know how to make it even better for you next time :)

Here's the link:

===>Click here to let us know

Best,
Amateo

Repurpose Your Summit Content!
Mastering content strategy, creation, and distribution for your brand on social media is a difficult and long process. But after hosting a virtual summit, you have in your hands over 20+ hours on content to dissect into hundreds of micro-content pieces ready to be distributed on social media.

Gary Vaynerchuk famously uses this strategy to create omnipresence for his digital marketing agency. The model works like this:

- Use one piece of "pillar content" (like an interview) and repurpose it into 30 other pieces of content designed to over index on the platforms they're meant to be distributed across.

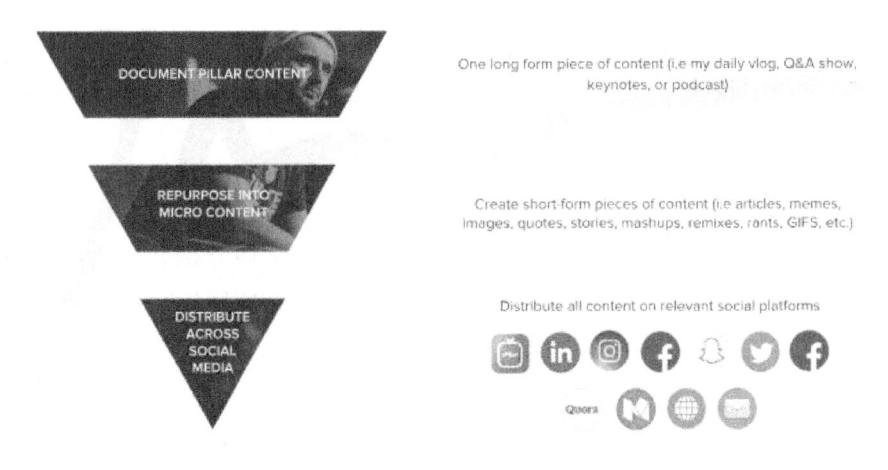

You might not have a videographer that follows you 18 hours a day (in fact you probably don't), but you *do* have a tremendous capital of content ready to be used on the internet.

1) **Facebook, Instagram, & Twitter Quotes**

Create quotes from your summit speakers on background images to make it visually appealing. These images can then be used to share on Facebook and

Instagram. If you have 20 interviews and get 5 quotes from each one of them, you will have 100 quotes ready to be promoted!

You can also ask your audience the sentence that made the most impact in their lives— and select them to be repurposed.

2) Write Blog Articles

Make sure to take the most important theme of each video and turn them into 500-1000 word articles. You can take the essentials and share the golden nuggets to your community. It will also help you build your SEO for your personal website.

Quora, Reddit, Medium, Linkedin, and Facebook are great distribution channels to promote your content. Add 1-3 major points to expand or articulate on something new. This makes the articles feel like new content and allows you to go deeper and rehash the ideas for your audience by adding even more value.

3) Write A Book

If you want to transcribe the majority of it, you can hire a virtual assistant to put all the interview into a book. Self-publishing through Amazon is a good solution, especially if you are interested in having a best-selling book in your niche. You will also have a community to promote your book to.

4) Launch A Podcast

I've shared many times in this book that you probably should not start a podcast if you want to solely generate revenue. But some people learn better through listening and might not always have the time to watch your videos.

Podcasts can be an incredible addition to your business to build authority. You can continue to interview industry experts via video, extract the MP3 from the recordings, and use it to launch a podcast. You can google different ways to have iTunes feature your podcast as new and noteworthy (similar strategy to becoming a best-selling author by becoming #1 in your category for a week).

You can also offer the video interviews as bonuses for customers who already bought your All-Access Pass.

5) Create Short Videos

You want to create a strong presence on every platform that your ideal audience spends time on. Not one. All of them. By having some 3-minute short clips (videos), a blog (writing), and a podcast (audio), you have 3 different strategies to drive traffic to your platform (virtual summit).

The best 15-second interview clips can also be used as an Instagram story to drive viewers back to the micro-content to increase engagement.

6) Write an Email Newsletter

Keep your community engaged by repurposing and sharing 1 lesson you learned from each interview to your list once a week. You can also periodically offer special recording discounts a couple weeks after the summit ends for those that haven't bought the All-Access Pass.

MAKING YOUR SUMMIT EVERGREEN

The evergreen summit feature is *one of the most powerful functions* to set up once your virtual summit ends. Evergreen summits allow for **ongoing lead generation plus profits by automating the summit to appear "Live" forever.**

In order words, it will appear to new visitors as if it is still getting ready to go live, and will still allow for new registrations. You can also set it up so that a summit displays the appropriate date automatically— without having to do anything afterwards.

Each new visitor goes through the same sequence, regardless of the day they opt in. Days and sessions are unlocked according to the system you've set up, then immediately lock down for anyone who hasn't upgraded, just like during the live summit.

The only thing that needs to be done is to after setting the technology side is managing your marketing budget.

A few additional reasons to transform your summit into an evergreen platform:
- Your Facebook ads pixel trackers are even more optimized to create look-alike audiences— resulting in cheaper cost per lead
- You help even more people reach their goal faster
- Your affiliates can continuously promote your summit (no need to have a specific launch date)
- You can design your marketing campaign to match your mastermind and retreat calendar

Although everyone can make their summit evergreen, I learned after helping a handful of clients that it works best when the summit content teaches timeless principles (e.g how to write and publish a book).

If your summit content needs to be updated every year because your industry changes so much (e.g Facebook ads), it might be more interesting to launch multiple smaller-scale summits.

It can also be a good idea to opt for an evergreen summit in between two launches to keep the engagement high.

(You can get your post-summit checklist on leadnextgen.com/book-bonus)

Relaunching Your Summit

If you don't want to turn your summit evergreen, re-launching the same summit in a few months can be another good option.

You can opt to treat your first summit like a beta test without investing much resources to gain confidence and understand how it can be made better. Launch at a small scale, stay within a comfortable budget, and work your way up to a big launch by adding more sophisticated options and improving your design.

You can also add more speakers and increase anticipation of your next launch by gathering metrics to share with new affiliates as a way to validate your offer.

Chapter 15: Let's Wrap it Up

Now that you've accessed **everything you need** to build and launch a wildly successful summit, it's time to put these tools into action.

By reading this book, **you've already taken the first step** toward distinguishing yourself from the unsatisfied masses by recognizing that our market demands content in more effective ways. You can be the one to deliver it.

And it doesn't have to be hard— you have in your hands the systematic breakdown of how to meet your summit goals. There's no excuse not to get started anymore.

But it requires action on your end. Limiting beliefs can prevent us from creating the reality we desire and deserve, especially if you wait too long. Take it from someone who used to be dragged down by them and managed to break free.

You can either sit back and watch as someone else employs the very tools you now know about, or you can **seize this success for yourself**. It's your choice.

People are achieving abundance with virtual summits, and even more to come, no questions asked. Here's the only part that needs answering: **is it going to be you?**

Printed in Great Britain
by Amazon